Aquafun
Volume 3: Playing and Training Creative

24 hour renewals and
information phoneline
020 8753 2400

Please return this book to any library
in the borough on or before the last
date stamped.
Fines are charged on overdue books.

Hammersmith
&Fulham
Serving our Community

AQUAFUN

PLAYING AND TRAINING CREATIVELY

UWE RHEKER

MEYER & MEYER SPORT

Original Title
Rheker, Uwe: Alle ins Wasser
Spielend schimmen – schwimmend spielen
Band 3: Kreativ und spielerisch trainieren
- Aachen: Meyer & Meyer, 2002

British Library Cataloguing in Publication Data
A catalogue record for this book is available from the British Library

Rheker, Uwe
Aquafun – Volume 3 Playing and Training Creatively
Oxford: Meyer & Meyer Sport (UK) Ltd., 2007
ISBN-10: 1-84126-184-X
ISBN-13: 978-1-84126-184-3

© 2007 by Meyer & Meyer Sport (UK) Ltd.
Aachen, Adelaide, Auckland, Budapest, Graz, Johannesburg, New York,
Olten (CH), Oxford, Singapore, Toronto
Member of the World
Sports Publishers' Association (WSPA)
www.w-s-p-a.org

Printed and bound by: FINIDR, s. r. o., Český Těšín
ISBN-10: 1-84126-185-8
ISBN-13: 978-1-84126-185-0
E-Mail: verlag@m-m-sports.com
www.m-m-sports.com

TABLE OF CONTENTS

FOREWORD

"When a stone falls into water
quite quietly and quite silently
despite it being ever so small
wide circles spread out a plenty"

(freely translated from a song by M. Siebald)

The environment of Water can be experienced in a number of various ways. The series of books, entitled "Aquafun - Learning by Playing" is designed to show the playful method of approaching learning to swim and move in water from a number of different aspects. Volume 1 (Aquafun - First Steps) concentrates mainly on "integrated concepts for beginner swimming" and shows a playful methodology for the development of swimming capability and skills, stretching from getting used to water up through to the introduction of the first swimming stroke techniques.

Volume 2, "Aquafun - Fun & Games for the Advanced" was devoted to the varied and rich palette of being able to move around playfully in water, once having learned to swim. Here, the main item was to show possibilities to impart the 'big games' in water (water polo, water basketball, water volleyball, underwater volleyball inter alia). Furthermore, quite new games were introduced such as water biathlon, aqua baseball etc., as well as covering the large field of 'little games' with various aims and forms of organization.

With the title of "Aquafun - Creative and Playful Swimming Training", the aim of Volume 3 is to conclude the trilogy with a work that shows how games and sport in the environment of water can be creatively and playfully put together. In Chapter 1 we show how this can be done by using various different pedagogical aspects. At the beginning of each of the sections in the chapter on exercises (Chapter 2) a few examples are introduced for the open creative approach to the aspects of diving underwater, jumping and diving in, life saving, artistic and synchronized swimming, aqua fitness and swimming training. This is done to make the swimming instruction and training successful with the various pedagogical aspects. There are severeal suggestions of games included, which should serve as a stimulus to develop further possibilities or which can be applied directly in exercising.

The fact that learning a technique can be accomplished by using games is clearly shown in the example of the introduction of the butterfly stroke in swimming (see Chapter 3).

My thanks go, first of all, to the Stiftung Westfalen (Germany) who have supported the project of "swimming as an integrative sport". *This has, amongst other things, allowed a databank containing numerous games and forms of exercise to be constructed for PC users – available only at the moment in the German language separate to this book series.* A special thanks goes to my scientific assistant Frank DUNSCHEN, who has contributed in a uniquely engaged manner to the work in enabling this book to be published. Moreover, he is the author of Chapters 2.2 and 2.6. For her productive encouragement in helping me to write Chapter 2.3, I would like to thank my colleague Christine THIELE (The Impulses for Creative and Playful Jumping and Diving into the Water). Thanks also goes to Dr. Harald REHN for his help with Chapter 2.4 "Life Saving". For his critical advice to the section on theory and editing the first chapter, I would like to heartily thank Karl-Heinz MÜCHER.

Paderborn – Summer 2006

Reflections on Playing in the Sport of Swimming

1

Playing and Water – An Introduction

1.1

"The sun will also cause a glint to shine from a tear"

(Maxi BÖHM)

Water is an element that is very closely related to life. At the same time it is also a symbol of life, because without water no life can exist: humans, animals and plants are all dependent on water.

Anyone, who has ever done a trek through the desert or has run in high temperatures, will know how significant, stimulating and refreshing water is. We come across water in various different forms:

➣ As water to drink from a cup to quench our thirst.

➣ As rain drops that fall on our faces or that water the dry earth.

➣ As a downpour from a tropical storm that clears the hot air.

➣ As a spring, stream, river, pond or lake. These areas of water illustrate water in its natural form: Spring water to drink and be refreshed, water in the lake or river to bathe and swim in.

➣ As a waterfall and as a wave breaking on the seashore where it demonstrates its forces to us.

➣ As steam in a gaseous form; climbing up hot from the earth and floating up as a cloud in the sky.

➣ As ice and snow with its hardness and coldness.

➣ Quite general as a poetic metaphor in lyrical texts.

➣ As a symbol of life in religious rituals.

Water, as a life-giving element, is also to be found in mineral springs. Enriched with minerals and other elements it helps to heal ill people. The holy rivers of the Jordan and the Ganges have also a cult meaning. To bathe in them is considered as cleansing the body and soul.

Water, as a necessity of life, implies moreover parallels and comparisons with our daily lives and social environment. We are all dependent on the next person as a social partner. Our fellow human beings are often like water, they are refreshing and invigorating. Sometimes, however, it can be like a cold November rain that slaps into our faces and chills us. We can find it obscure and frightening like a dark, soupy and impenetrable lake in a wood surrounded by high fir trees, so that hardly any light falls on it. The first large snowflakes can lie softly on our hands like the gentle touch of a person lovingly stroking us.

Water also brings danger with it: with downhill torrents, flooding and storm tides, it can show us the force of water. By analogy this can be compared to the brutality of our fellow humans in war, crime, terror acts and repression.

The refreshing bath after a long hike, swimming in the early morning hours in an open-air swimming pool after a late night out, wakens our senses. Similarly a cheerful person can invigorate us and get us going all day.

Water has a lot of different meanings to many of us and can be a companion for us, all of our lives.

Taking account of all these semantic references, this book is designed to open up the environment of water as a place to move round in and, inter alia, provide the creative and playful development of the various aspects of swimming.

In order to symbolize once again the extensive importance of water, in conclusion, I would like to tell a story about the subject of water. A story can, as is true of fairy tales, have complex and deep, abstract definitional meanings. Definitions and philosophical considerations call for an understanding intellect. On the other hand, fairy tales and stories appeal to other levels in human beings; the emotions, fantasy, dreams, feelings and sensitivities. A story has better expressiveness of playing in water than any abstract definitions. Therefore, here is a little story as an introduction to the subject of water.

The Two Blocks of Ice

Once upon a time there were two blocks of ice. The relationship between them was very cool, which isn't at all surprising. One of them thought: Why doesn't the other one come any nearer to me? But the blocks of ice couldn't come and go. Then one of them thought: If the other one melts, then I will also melt. The block of ice could not melt on its own, so neither of them melted.

And so it came to pass that no one came nearer and each of them got more and more icy. After a few months - or was it years? - one of the blocks of ice discovered at midday as the sun shone that he was melting and he saw that he was turning into water. The other one also had the same experience. They floated together in the natural causeway between them. They met. They still felt their coldness, but they also felt their weaknesses and their goodwill, they felt each their own necessity and that of the other. They found that they needed each other and that they would have to stay together.

And then a child came along, and another, and yet more children. And they let their little toy boats float on the great strong water. The blocks of ice heard the children playing happily. And this happiness was reflected in itself just like the sun on the water.

P. CORNELIS
(JAKOBI 1981, 11)

1.2 The Importance of Playing and Games in Water

"Joy is the spring, from which our lives are refreshed and revived"

Hans MÜHLE

1.2.1 The General Importance of Playing

Games have a particular importance for the development of youngsters growing up. The basic importance of playing in a world, characterized by work, school, profession and the earnestness of life is without doubt indisputable. Some of the general assessments and characteristic features regarding the philosophy of playing and the games are listed in the following passages:

Playing can be antipodal to work and serve as a balance against the trials and tribulations met in the working world.

➢ Playing is an activity, which occurs purely from the joy in doing it.

➢ Playing, as a simple activity and alternative paradigm to worldly matters, serves to give relaxation. As a result games and playing in your free time take on a special importance.

➢ Playing means, particularly for the generation of growing children, practicing behavioral patterns and having the opportunity to learn creatively.

➢ Playing gives adolescents the opportunity to come to terms with their material and social environment.

➢ Children must be given the opportunity to be able to collect basic playing experiences. Sports clubs often make the mistake by concentrating on training too early in the specific sports subjects. SCHMIDT (1993, p 24) rightly complains that there is a tendency to "train" children "before they have learned to play on their own".

➢ By playing in groups adolescents learn how to keep to rules of the game that it can succeed. This capability is also important in daily routine and in the social community.

➤ Free and experimental playing can encourage the creativity of young people.

These different levels of importance take on various aims (RHEKER 2005, "Aquafun - Games and Fun for the Advanced" pp 13-25). Games broaden the sphere of experiences and take on new areas of one's environment.

Creative play opens up possibilities to play to rules and give the opportunity to develop one's own rules. In the official game of water polo is not a lot opportunity to be that creative, but in the areas of 'little games' and little sports matches this is quite possible.

Particularly during swimming lessons for beginners there will be several opportunities to 'play' with the rules. Here, games can be varied or new games 'invented'.

When children are asked to develop their own rules of a game, they can be very creative. Therefore, particularly during swimming instruction, sufficient time and free playing periods should be allowed, or even set as tasks, to allow the children to take part in developing ideas for games and creativity.

Children come to terms with their environment by playing. They try out the possibilities on their own e.g., to try to move around in water. By subjectively analysing the element water, children make new experiences, which were not possibly on dry land (buoyancy, floating, moving in three dimensions etc.). New areas to move in must be opened up for the children. "Areas to move perceived as real areas are areas of perceiving possibilities to act." (LOIBL 1992, p 29).

The playful and subjective approach to the environment of water can be opened up by using freedom of tasks and methods:

➤ Moving around in water with and without contact with the bottom of the pool.

➤ Diving by sinking in water.
➤ Using buoyancy and floating without sinking in water.
➤ Moving creatively to music in water.
➤ Entering the water creatively, doing funny jumps into the water.

Because of this fact, each chapter with exercises in this book is begun with such creative play (see Chapters 2.1. - 2.7.).

Playing in Different Places
You can play practically everywhere. Children already have their first play experiences in the home environment, in the living room or the children's room. They get to learn their first proper games in the playgroup or kindergarten. Sports games are possible in the gymnasium, in the swimming hall and on the sports pitch. However, it is also possible to play games in the open air, in woods, on fields, in and on the sea and many other places.

Water – a Space to Move Around in
The environment of water offers unique possibilities for us to be able to make movements and have experiences, which are not imaginable or even possible on dry land. Buoyancy, which the body experiences in water, makes it possible to experience weightlessness. Water permits almost complete weightless movements to be made in three dimensions. This is something that has only been possible for astronauts in space.

Even as a baby we have had experiences of swimming and diving in the amniotic sac inside our Mother's womb. As a result babies already feel 'at home' in water and are able to swim at an early age (c.f., RHEKER 2004, "Aquafun - First Steps" p 77).

Water permits a special experience for the body. Our bodies can float in water and are completely lapped around by the element of water. In water we can perceive our environment more directly tactile than on dry land. We can feel the warmth or the coldness of the water more intensively, because water, as a medium, has a much greater capability to conduct temperature.

When swimming, playing or diving in and under water, we can perceive further things that are quite 'unique'. Thus, when we look around under water without diving goggles it is all blurred. However, when we use either swimming or diving goggles, we can make out things much clearer and larger, and for example, we can see the wonders of the underwater world when diving in tropical waters.

Our hearing is also changed because of the higher density of water. Sounds can be perceived more directly and over greater distances. It is an enjoyable, but not easy task to recognize songs being sung underwater. Vocal exchanges, though, are difficult if hardly understandable. This is why divers have developed a sign language offering new realms of communication (see Chapter 2.1.).

Water is an environment for all target groups
Children in all ages, from babies up through infancy, pre-school age, school children and youths (teens and twenties), grown-ups at all stages of life (also older people, who find the going on dry land difficult because of a physical disability), all can move in water in a "fleet-footed" manner.

People with varying degrees of capability can be active together in water gymnastics, aqua jogging, swimming for fun and playing around in the water etc.

Social status and social barriers, which are manifested in the clothing one wears and other similar status symbols have no effect in water since everyone is "in their bathing suits". In water everyone is the same!

Disabled people of all categories can move about on their own independently in water without aids such as crutches or wheelchairs.
    This is why playing and moving about in water is very suitable for people of different capabilities to be able to join together actively and experience things together, see "Swimming as an Integrative Sport" (in Chapter 1.5 and RHEKER, 2004, "Aquafun - First Steps" pp 42-67).

1.2.2   The Importance of Games in the Water

Swimming and playing in water is popular in all social spheres. Empirical studies on the sporting interests of young people have shown that swimming and playing in water is right at the top of the popularity scale.

According to a study done by BRETTSCHNEIDER/BRÄUTIGAM (1990), the sport of swimming is the sport mostly carried out in all spheres of activity - including the family sphere, in free time and in 'cliques' of the same age (1990, pp58-62). The same kind of result was found by BRETTSCHNEIDER/KRAMER, 1978; SACK, 1985; VELTINS Sports Study 2001 inter alia. In Germany, the principle importance of swimming for disabled youngsters, as they grow up, is described in the BRETTSCHNEIDER/RHEKER Study (1996), commissioned by the German State of North Rhine Westphalia's Ministry of Culture.

The report said that the sport of swimming was in first place for disabled children and youths, clearly ahead of other types of sport including those carried out actively in a club or during leisure time as well as those held as a favorite sport (c.f., BRETTSCHNEI-DER/RHEKER, 1996 pp45-49; RHEKER, 1996c, pp62-76).

The high degree of popularity decreases, however, as people get older. A contributory factor to this phenomenon is that swimming, following on from the varied and playful beginner swimming training in school and club, is often limited to swimming in lanes. The varied experience and activities possible when playing and romping around in water during one's leisure time, should be included and retained in swimming instruction in schools.

Therefore, it is hoped that this book will give a stimulus on how the environment of water can be used to achieve differing aims and possibilities for creative and playful movement in water.

A discussion on the various meanings of moving about and playing in water has been covered comprehensively in Volume 2 (RHEKER, 2005 (Aquafun - Games and Fun for the Advanced). Before going on to give practical examples, we start with a portrayal of the various aims attributable for games in the water.

By abandoning the rather technical interpretation of the term 'swimming', whereby this is understood as being movement in one of the four Olympic swimming styles and techniques in straight lanes in a standard-sized pool, we open up a variety of different aspects. Swimming is a varied 'self-exercise' activity in, by, into and under water (c.f., SCHERLER, 1981). Taking all of this one step further, it gives us another way of tackling the experiences of *the environment of water* individually.

Thus the interpretation of the complexes presented in the following passages must be seen as a framework, in which the individual - whether he is a beginning swimmer, an advanced swimmer, the water polo player, the diver etc., - can try out his own way of moving and playing in water. As a result, this introduces a "subjective analysis process with the environment of water" (HILDEBRANDT, 1993, p 199), and this brings a new element in which to move, and a variety of possibilities to learn, play and move in, by, into and under water.

The meanings attributed can be easily explained in a few key words.

Fun/Enjoyment
The dominating motive for sporting activity, and this includes the sport of swimming, is for disabled and non-disabled children and youngsters **to have fun** (c.f., BRETTSCHNEIDER/BRÄUTIGAM, 1990, p54; BRETTSCHNEIDER/RHEKER, 1996, p41; RHEKER, 1996b, p103).

Experiencing the Body
Swimming and playing activities in the water give one a particular awareness of the body. The medium of water, with the specific characteristics of density and the pressure exerted by it, the buoyancy and its conductivity of temperature, gives a person a particular awareness of his physique.

Movement in water gives all people spatial experiences, which on dry land would partly be beyond them. In this way one can float in water and move in three dimensions, roll-over in different directions just as you like, do somersaults, do screw like movements rolling the body over, tipping movements up and down, or even combinations of these movements like in the sideways screw somersault (see Chapter 2.3.). One can train one's coordination ability particularly well.

When swimming, playing and training in water, you can feel the strain on the body very directly. Tiredness, but also relaxation and recuperation can be intensively felt (c.f., in particular Chapter 2.6 "Aqua Fitness and Aqua Wellness").

Independence

Learning to swim on one's own is a very significant step in the development of the personality of a young person.

By learning to swim, one has "swum free" from the supervision of grown-ups. A new environment can be conquered. Now that you have more confidence, this kind of independence means more self-assurance and self-confidence.

The variety of possibilities now open to you in water, by the water, into the water and under water, with or without equipment, not only permits different movement experiences, but also fosters the development of creativity and ideas, as well as self-realization.

Health

Health, fitness, relaxation all belong to the complex of motives that have a large importance in swimming, playing and moving in water. This is why the terms *health promotion and development of health awareness* have a particular value in moving about in the water.

The mental side of the term health can be described using emotional situations; well being, fearlessness, relaxed state, security, fun. Here, fun and joy, which one can display when playing and swimming in water, lead to harmony in breaking down inner tensions. This psychosomatic regulation can be aimed at and achieved by doing relaxation training and water gymnastics. By being in the water and moving about in it, one's general state of health can be improved and one can achieve an intensive feeling in the body. The particular areas of Aqua Fitness and Aqua Wellness are devoted to achieving this state. However, a quiet long stamina swim can also improve the general state of mind considerably.

Experiences with Equipment

Water permits specific experience of the equipment being used. Just by being in water we learn about the characteristics of water in a very close aspect. Water is wet, and because of its high degree of conductivity, we can differentiate between warmth and coldness more directly and clearly. Water gives in, but it also offers resistance. Water is soft to the touch, but it also can be relatively hard, for example, when you land on your back from a dive into the water.

Playing Games

Those adolescents experience the environment of water in a playful manner. The full variety of games for use on, in, and under water is covered in the three volumes "Aquafun - Learning by Playing" (RHEKER, 2004, 2005, 2006).

Leisure Sports

Swimming and playing in water using various ways of moving opens up the opportunity to do many sporting and leisure oriented activities:

> Swimming is an ideal stamina sport, which can be carried out by any age group.
> A variety of movements are possible:
  From the four main swimming styles up through to innumerous creative or individual techniques of moving forward.

Movements in water can be shaped

> From simple jumping in feet first through to popular diving up to artistic diving and high board diving.
> From simple movements to music up to artistic and synchronized swimming. Movements in water can be done to music.

One can play in water

From simple running and catching games through to relay races, little ball games right up to the big games:

> Water polo, water football, water basketball, water rugby, water volleyball, water biathlon, underwater polo.
> Snorkelling and diving.
> Health opportunities in water:
> Water gymnastics, spinal cord gymnastics, aqua jogging, aqua wellness etc.

Performance/Competition

Swimming and playing in water can be done from the aspect of performance and improving performance. The improvement of performance can not only be achieved by carrying out the usual training forms. There is a multitude of creative games and playful exercises also available.

Aesthetics, Form

For swimming, within the meaning of these terms, it is all to do with the particular quality of how the movement is executed, how the movement is presented and how the body flows during the movement. In the sport of swimming, this happens, in particular, in springboard and high diving, artistic and synchronized swimming and in the so-called "perfection swimming".

Adventure, Risk, Tension

In many situations in swimming, when diving underwater or diving in, tension is created where the outcome of such situations is uncertain. Therefore many aspects of the sport of swimming can be labeled and linked to adventure, risk and responsibility.

Prevention/Rehabilitation

Sport from the aspect of **Prevention or Rehabilitation** is closely related to the meaning of the terms health, fitness or compensating relaxation. Special sporting activity can be a prophylactic against illnesses caused by a lack of exercise such as a heart attack or danger of one, fatty liver condition, overweight etc.

Equally, deliberate gymnastics and swimming, in particular the backstroke can contribute in compensating against posture and back problems as well as reducing weaknesses or even heal them.

Social Experiences

In particular, playing in water is a sporting activity that permits special social experiences. Games make communication and social interaction all the easier (see "Communicative Games", RHEKER 2005, "Aquafun - Games and Fun for the Advanced", pp 55-63).

When swimming and playing in the water, the differences between young and old people, between people with or without disabilities are not so great. People of varying abilities can get into the act together. This is why the social motive with disabled children and youths is particularly important (c.f., RHEKER, 1996b, p103).

Social integration can be achieved in a sports group by taking part in joint activities. This fact can be put to use in a number of ways also in swimming. This is because swimming, with its variety of movement possibilities, offers a rich palette of activities for even people, who because of their various disabilities would not be able to take part in such events on dry land.

Particularly, the areas of aqua fitness, aqua jogging and swimming as a hobby offer a variety of movement forms with the aim of prevention of injury, rehabilitation and social integration.

Games in Sports Training and Swimming Instruction

1.3

"Movement is the sustenance of life"

Martin BUBER

First of all, a review of the progress in didactics will show how swimming instruction has been developed in latter years, in order to make it clear how the shift of accent has been incorporated in the lesson planning that now takes place.

Here, we will consider what the pedagogical basis is that produces **a modern idea of swimming instruction,** and how it can be structured under various aspects. This is followed by consideration of what value **swimming** and **playing in water** has in lesson planning.

A Didactical Review of Swimming

1.3.1

In the course of history, swimming and swimming instruction has been viewed with various different meanings. Based on the educational system in Germany, and the same might be true in other countries, the following traces that course:

- Sports instruction (physical education in schools) was orientated in the 60s mainly towards common types of sport. Swimming instruction at this time was only considered as being about the four Olympic disciplines and swimming was reduced to being done in lanes.

- By the middle of the 70s, instruction in swimming was divided into three levels of objectives (c.f., WILKE/FASTRICH 1972) where the first phase was devoted to beginners' swimming with getting familiar and coming to terms with water being the main aims. This moved on then to instruction on the techniques (breast, crawl, back crawl and butterfly strokes). The third level of objectives then made use of these techniques in the various different types of water sports: competitive sports swimming, water polo games, sports underwater diving, artistic forms of swimming, life saving and high board diving. Many children don't find this form of swimming and instruction much fun because it is too one-sided and relates too much to the norms of competitive swimming and is too performance-based.

- From the middle of the 70s, sports and swimming instruction became more freely constructed. Variety in sports and the different motives to do sport were brought more to the fore when considering educational needs. The individual's ability to act is underlined. The guidelines laid down in Germany (North Rhine Westphalia) in 1980 show swimming as a sporting event where one can experience all its various forms. This educational basic had not been sufficiently abundant in the way the concrete recommendations for instruction had been interpreted (c.f., KURZ 2000, p 10).

Didactic references to swimming

- G. VOLCK set new yardsticks for swimming instruction in his book. Swimming instruction should initiate the following educational references in its various forms for schoolchildren:
  - Swimming allows one to experience in particular the body and the environment.
  - Swimming increases the ability to act, increases independence and self-confidence.
  - Swimming embraces a new social environment and allows particular social experiences.

- Swimming can be healthy.
- Swimming affords elements of creativity or representation of movement.
- Moving about in water can be done to rules and elements of games can be integrated in it.
- Swimming can also be a competitive sport (c.f., KURZ/VOLCK 1977, pp 47-54).

These didactic references and interpretations to swimming can be extended upon in the argument for the cause of varying beginners' swimming instruction and employing an integrated concept for beginners' swimming (c.f., RHEKER 1999a, pp 14-24).

- Fun
- Health
- Experiencing the body
- Particular awareness
- Experience equipment and material
- Social experience
- Independence
- Life saving

- Playing
- Performance, competition
- Leisure activity – leisure sports
- Aesthetics, creativity
- Adventure, risks, excitement
- preventative health measure/ Rehabilitation
- Portal to the world of water sports

In Germany, in the revision of the school curriculum for North Rhine Westphalia (Land Institute for Schools and Further Education 1999/2000), these interpretations for sports were collected together into six educational basic principles. These allowed the use of a varied swimming instruction method in different aspects to be achieved.

Pedagogical Basics   1.3.2

For the "Educational basic principles of the North Rhine Westphalian curriculum revision", KURZ (2000) introduced basic principles, which were generally conceived for school sports, but which are also suitable at the same time for a varied instruction method in a variety of areas for swimming. In a development of the physical educational concept from 1980, the German Schools Program Commission selected six educational aspects.

Educational aspects can be seen as certain viewpoints, which are taken into account when putting together sport or swimming (in this case) instruction. Some overlapping is more than likely to happen. "Each aspect stems from a particular viewpoint, as to what sporting activities can be educationally useful" (KURZ 2000, p 25). In doing this the individual interpretation can be used. The schoolchildren (infants, youths and older participants etc.,) should be brought on from where they stand with their expectations and previous experiences.

The cultivation of the ability to act on the part of the children can be reached on two planes: They have to learn to be able to take part in sport with competence and develop the ability "to see sport with some meaning and structure it this way" (KURZ 2000, p 14).

One speaks of a dual task for sports instruction, which on the one hand is a question of promoting the development of the individual and on the other hand it should embrace the "meaning of the cultural phenomenon of sport" (KURZ 2000, p 27).

Educational aspects stem from an open understanding of the sport. They formulate what the children do, experience or learn:

1. To improve the ability to be aware, develop experiences in movements.
2. To be able to express oneself with the body and create movements.
3. To be adventurous and yet responsible.
4. To experience being able to perform something, understand it and be able to judge correctly.
5. To be able to cooperate, be competitive and be able to communicate.
6. Promote health and develop health-consciousness.

1 To improve the ability to be aware, develop experiences in movements.

Learning with all the senses was emphasized already by Maria MONTESSORI (1870-1952) as a principle of holistic education. As a result of a failure to activate themselves and a lack of motivation to exercise, many adolescents indicate deficiencies in the areas of movement experience and coordination ability. This is reflected in the latest tests for ADS syndrome[1] (Attention Deficit Syndrome) and the interdependence between the senses and brain activity. The motor pedagogic and the psychomotor attempt to balance these deficits by promoting a childlike development (c.f., KIPHARD 1990; 1992; IRMISCHER 1980; ZIMMER/CICURS 1992 inter alia).

Motor pedagogic represents a holistic promotion, which has the aim of furthering the development of the whole personality by using the motor sense.

In this, the unit of movement and perceptiveness is underlined. The world is revealed to the human being through movement. He discovers his identity by experiencing and recognizing the functions and actions of his own body. By using the hands and generally understanding what is happening, the child learns to come to terms with its body and to build concepts. In this way, movement is the basic element for cognitive development.

The ability to perceive will generally be improved and developed by tasks that address the various senses. The various experiences with the senses are transmitted via the specific type of sense: optical, acoustical, tactile, vestibular and kinesthetic experiences of the body and spatial feelings.

By the improvement of perception and the ability to process the individual impressions of sense and experience, the young person learns more about himself and at the same time, he learns about the "materiel environment" (c.f., SCHERLER 1975). In this way he develops different patterns of perception. By relating to the patterns of perception, which are being continually extended and interrelated, he learns to orient himself and be in a position to be able to react with the correct motor sense.

In particular, moving about in water allows various experiences to be made via the different senses:

Feeling
Via the irritation of the skin, various feelings can be perceived and distinguished: The coldness of water, gliding through the water, submerging in water, water resistance, water pressure when diving underwater etc.

---

1 The ADS syndrome is characterized by short periods of inattentiveness, impulsive, uncontrolled behavior and in many cases hyperactive behavior.

Visual experiences

There are optical impressions of the size of the swimming pool or of open water. One perceives third dimensions; e.g., when diving, playing underwater ball games etc.

Equilibrium experiences

When you move against the resistance of the water, like trying to walk through waves, you can try to maintain your balance or be swept along in the stream. One can also make vestibular experiences of the senses in a playful manner and by not letting yourself be put off balance or by regaining your balance once lost.

Movements and kinesthetics

Kinesthetic experiences can be made in situations e.g., when you are lying relaxed on top of the water or when you tense or relax your body (c.f., "Aqua Wellness" Chapter 2.6). Movement experiences can be further developed when trying out new techniques e.g., doing the butterfly stroke, artistic and synchronized swimming or when diving in headfirst.

Hearing

The hearing is different underwater than on dry land. When under a shower, sounds come over differently. This is why some like to sing when having a bath or a shower.

Taste and Smell

The taste and smell of water tell us something about its quality.

A further principle of the psychomotor system and other holistic concepts of development have been shown in the improvement of the ability to perceive. Experiencing a variety of movement experiences has priority over specialization at a stage which is far too early and priority over the single-track learning of techniques. Carrying out freely chosen movements allows more varied experiences of movement, freely chosen play and creative motion structures.

Motor pedagogic and the psychomotor system realize in this an implicitly fun-making, pleasure-seeking development and both playfully allow, by means of motor processes, successful movement and social experiences.

This way of learning to move should - and this is logically clear from the passages already mentioned - find a way into every form of sport and swimming instruction. This is because these movement experiences create the basis for learning more movements, learning techniques in the various types of sport and also tuition in the cognitive disciplines.

Experiences of freely chosen movements also develop inter alia the ability to coordinate, without which no one can become a good athlete.

2. To be able to express oneself with the body and create movements. Our body is also an instrument, with which we express ourselves. In this way we can see from body language whether someone is sad, tired or happy. Particularly for children or disabled persons, who cannot speak or who have limited command of language, body language is an important medium for communication. "The concept of the body is an important part of the alter ego, particularly being vital for the development in later child and adolescent years" (KURZ 2000, p 30).

Regarding this aspect, it is important that we experience our own ability to move and our own ability to express ourselves with our bodies as well as improve this feature and put it to use. In particular, one can learn to accept oneself, the body and its capabilities, increase its expression and thus develop the personality.

When sports and swimming instruction is planned with this aspect in mind, it is all to do with a form of aesthetic upbringing where the quality of the movement is in the foreground. Movements of this nature can be beautiful, expressive or impressive. The so-called *movement arts* serve as examples of this. This doesn't mean that they have to be done like a circus act, but rather it is sufficient to do them simply and individually as a sort of trick turn, which the actor can do for fun.

The spectrum of the types of sport, which are subjects in this aspect, is very large. Besides the traditional aesthetic oriented types of sport like exercising, gymnastics, figure skating, springboard and high-board diving, artistic and synchronized swimming etc., there are also the motions involved in acrobatics, juggling, skating, trick skiing and movement theater. KURZ (2000, p 30) developed four considerations of educational value for movement experiences under these aspects:

- **"Play with the variety of human movement"** leads to the development of the personality of the child and to the increase of creativity in sporting activity.

- **"Movement as a driver in being brought up aesthetically"** develops movement capabilities that are discovered by children when playing freely and by experimenting with new movements, which is seen impressively in games such as skateboard acrobatics. In this it is often the subjective impression that is the important thing, and not the objective performance criteria.

- **"Movement as an expression of individuality":** By using body expressions, each person develops his individuality, his unique personality features. By the way they move, one can recognize people. However, you can also read how they are feeling by watching the way they move. A person who is sad will move differently to a happy one.

- **"Movement as a medium for communication and companionship":** We can express a lot with our movements, which cannot be turned into words. This form of communication is particularly important for people, who are only able to communicate verbally on a limited basis, like mentally disabled children for example.

The communicative importance of movement can have an effect on improving companionship when movement takes place in a joint environment, such as social dancing sessions or in synchronized swimming. Particularly in the movement arts and when discovering new movements as a group, this element takes on the character of improving integration:

The different movements found in the various cultures of the various nationalities in a class can be turned into themes. Using the title of "National Games", the different cultural aspects and games of people from other nations can lead to new movement experiences (c.f., RHEKER 1994).

3   To be adventurous and yet responsible.

This aspect includes the interpretation of *adventure, risk and excitement* but goes far beyond these things. In many sporting situations we experience excitement, because the outcome is not certain. There are so many game situations where the result is undecided for a long time, such as in an exciting game of football or water polo. A different type of excitement can be created, if the situation is connected with a risk because for us a new stimulus is now involved - the stimulus of the unknown. Sometimes we decide ourselves to enter an unsure situation, so that we can overcome the challenge. In this way, and with mixed feelings, a non-swimmer lifts his feet off the bottom of the pool for the first time. Similarly, the first time one goes diving with an aqualung or makes the first dive from the 10-meter board create emotions in us ranging between anxiousness and the thrill of expectation.

Judging risk and danger is experienced subjectively and very differently between people. Individually, but also between people, risk can be felt as an emotion between caution and despondency up to temerity. The same situation leads children in the same class to display different reactions such as seen in the simple example of jumping from a springboard; some children throw themselves in daringly from the diving board while others shy away from it and don't have the confidence to jump in.

Risk is a typical factor of many situations in sport. Whenever new situations crop up in sport for the first time, they can be seen as constituting a risk. In this, individual ability and experience play a decisive role. It depends whether we can get round something through having done it routinely, or simply see ourselves being confronted unexpectedly with new challenges. However, what lies behind the reasons for the desire to experience life at the limits in so-called extreme sports is a subject that needs to be addressed, in my opinion, in the form of a separate theoretical study based on social behavior.

Whenever we have conquered a difficult situation, we can be proud of our capabilities. Conquering situations regarding challenges met when moving about help children to discover themselves and this leads to gaining more confidence. They learn to be able to judge their own abilities realistically and use these correctly in the appropriate situation.

KURZ speaks of three aspects why risk in sport is valuable:

> "for someone, who ventures to the limits of his own capabilities, and under certain circumstances, goes beyond those" (KURZ 2000, p37). This is a matter of the motor abilities and skills, but also whenever one is confronted by anxiousness on the psychic level.

> "for someone, who takes a risk purely on the basis of using his own judgement of his ability in a realistic manner" (KURZ 2000, p 37). Confidence in one's own ability can be strengthened in a situation where a risk is being taken. This serves to increase one's self-esteem.

> Many situations in sport can only be ventured when one has to be able to rely on others. Now, the reliability of others has to be added to one's own abilities. This comes over clearly in the supporting role given in gymnastics when relying on a partner, when aqualung diving or when relying on a safety man when climbing. Furthermore social responsibility is put particularly to the test in for example life saving.

4 To experience being able to perform something, understand it and be able to judge correctly

Sport is nearly always closely connected with the interpretation of the term *performance*. To be able to reach a certain performance means that one develops one's own ability or develops it further. For the improvement of one's own performance, practice plays a decisive role. Without practice and training the performance ability cannot be improved. Social recognition of performance, particularly for the achievement of a high degree of performance, is very high and thus increases motivation.

Judging performance in sport appears to be simple. Children can often judge performance spontaneously. They do not always consider the absolute performance as the central element, but more often it is the individual achievement that is important.

The educational task of a performance-oriented upbringing has, for KURZ (2000, p38 et seq.), the following main emphasis:

> Movement, games and sports increase the confidence in one's own ability to perform. This is where young people learn that by practicing and training you can improve your performance. At the

same time self-confidence is increased and this has a positive effect on other matters in life.

➤ Because performance pressure can also lead to failure, the interrelation between performance and self-esteem is ambivalent. For this reason, instructors, trainers and exercise leaders have to treat the assessment of performance with care, and for example, take note of the various performance prerequisites. Similarly, recognition of the performance of others must also be given. Team performance also furthers social experiences in this way.

➤ From experience in sports instruction we know that performance alone has no objective or absolute value. "The assessment [of performance]... is based on the agreement over quality criteria and rules" (KURZ 2000, p39). One performance can be compared with an earlier one achieved or with how others have done.

5   To be able to cooperate, be competitive and able to communicate
Sport is not simply an area where the only thing measured is the competitive prowess. Movement, games and sport makes the coming together of people with different conditions possible and lays the foundation, in which social relationships and good social behavior can flourish. Movement, games and sport generate, almost on their own, an intensive feeling for community and public spirit. This is one of the main motives for many people in joining a sports club. In a world, where people mix little, they seek company and social enjoyment, also through sport and in doing it.

In sport, it is easy to come into contact with others, striking up conversations and experiencing communication with them. Little games with the emphasis on communication are particular suitable for this (c.f., RHEKER 2005 (Aquafun - Games and Fun for the Advanced), pp 55-62). Because the language of sport is international, this helps in breaking down the communication barrier. This was experienced in our family integrated sports groups, in which primarily, people with and without disabilities played sport together, and where we were able to also integrate children of other nationalities (c.f., RHEKER, 1996b, p 80). Although, at the beginning, these children understood hardly any German, they were able to spontaneously take part without any problem, because they were able to grasp the idea of the game quickly. This proves one of the reasons why movement, games and sport are particularly suitable to use in integrating disabled persons and non-nationals (see also Chapter 1.5 "Swimming as an integrative Sport").

Equally, sport offers the possibility to interact with people. That is to say, beyond the aspects of communication into the realm of developing a socially defined way of acting. The environment of water is particularly good for the joint interactivity of different people (c.f., RHEKER 2005 (Aquafun - Games and Fun for the Advanced), pp 63-66). Movement, games and sport show us that it is better to act together rather than use force against another person. In sport, it is possible to experience, in a playful manner, how social cooperation functions and how social problems can be solved.

Picture 1: Cooperation and competition while jousting piggy-back

The German Schools Program Commission tried to bring these pedagogical aspects onto three levels, where the aspects were particularly relevant to the social processes in sport and swimming instruction (c.f., KURZ 2000, p 40 et seq.).

> **Following rules and adapting them**
Sports and games, from little games up to the major sports, all follow agreed set rules. In this way, children can learn how to keep to the rules in sport and in games, i.e., they develop a sense for the 'rule regime'. At the same time, they are able to adapt to rules for the prevailing situation, as is the case in the little games. Thus they learn to develop rules, adapt them further and even make up new games with their own rules.

> **Being brought up to be independent and socially responsible**
There are many situations in sports where youngsters growing up experience the impulse to be independent. This is particularly noticeable when learning to swim and learning to dive. At the same time, however, social responsibility has to be adopted, because these new situations can only often happen with the help of others, such as occurs in life saving or joint cooperation in group activities such as artistic swimming and synchronized swimming, for example.

> **Differences in individuals**
Sport brings all sorts of different people together. Young and old, boys and girls, disabled people and able-bodied people, people of different nationalities and people from all walks of life etc., can come together like this. Integrative sport shows us that here is an opportunity to integrate and to learn about the society on several levels around us (c.f., RHEKER 1996b, pp44-52 & pp62-82). The cultural variety, which can be found in schools today, also offers an opportunity to enrich movement and sports instruction by virtue of the cultural differences each brings with him.

6 To promote health and develop health-consciousness
To all appearances, there is a clear connection between movement, games and sport and the aspects of health. Many people join a sports club or go to a fitness studio in order to do something for their health. A lack of movement activity is the most common cause of many illnesses. One sees between 50-65% of the children appearing with symptoms of inactivity (poor posture, overweight, signs of coordination difficulties etc). This also has an effect on health in schoolwork (c.f., DORDEL 1993, p143).

Health risks are also prevalent in grown-ups and older people when they don't exercise sufficiently. Movement, games and sport give us - also in a compensating sense - a good respect for our bodies and permit us to lead a healthy lifestyle. For children, who follow their natural urge to move, the idea of respect for the body, so to speak, is inborn. However, if even after the end of the first school year they are taught to sit still instead of following their natural instinct to be on the move, then their natural urge to be active will be impaired. A stifling of activity will inevitably result in tension.

In order to compensate for the negative effects of a lack of movement activity, school lessons, even in theoretical subjects such as languages, arithmetic and mathematics etc., can incorporate elements to cover moving about where these meet the children's requirements. Doing deliberate movement exercises and sporting activities relieves stress and tension and improves the well being of the body.

A healthy lifestyle, which includes movement exercises, also contributes to strengthening of one's self-esteem. Most sporting activities take place in groups. The social contact that springs from this is also important for the physical and mental well being. Movement activity should not be carried out if injuries exist. Besides those projects fostered by the health authorities, movement, games and sport also represent a pillar for the prevention of illnesses. Games and sports are great fun. The joy in carrying out physical activity and movement should be a good reason for bringing movement and sport into the daily routine. The emphasis on movement, games and sport, thus achieved, will allow us to lead a healthy life.

1.3.3 The Different Aspects of Sports Training and Swimming Instruction

Sports instruction that seeks to fulfill the various different pedagogical aims must display all the aspects. If it adequately covers all the various possibilities, it will influence the structure of the student's motivation more intensively, and in turn, bring many people to follow a long-term lifestyle where movement is the center point.

There is no form of sport that has only one purpose. The form is "always part of the purpose" (KURZ 2000, p 46). Thus, activities from the various areas of sport can cover the purpose in different ways. In this way, artistic and high diving can be brought together to relate with the pedagogical aspects:

- **Expanding movement experiences:** In diving, new movement sequences are learned e.g., a twisting somersault.
- **To express oneself physically, making movements:** While in the air, one can do movements that are very expressive and impress others.
- **Daring to do something on one's own:** The first time you jump from the springboard or dive from the high board poses a risk and demands will-power and courage. This is particularly so from heights such as cliff-diving.
- **Experiencing one's performance and understanding it and gauging it:** After doing a successful, or even an unsuccessful dive one can clearly judge that performance oneself.
- **Showing cooperation, competing and communicating:** This aspect is clearly prevalent in competitive situations, but can also be experienced when diving together with someone and in group activities when diving.

So that the instruction in the various areas of swimming instruction is carried out with the whole palette of the pedagogic practice in mind, at the beginning of each chapter, several examples of how to approach this are included.

1.4 The Essential Elements of Swimming and Games in the Water

*"Everything, in so far as it is in itself,
endeavors to persist in its own being"*

Baruch Benedictus de SPINOZA

The variety we meet in games, particularly those called 'little games', also gives us a plethora of variable ways that these games can be used i.e., games can be used with very many different aims in mind for sport and swimming instruction.

Based on the pedagogic aspects (see previous), the playful and creative way of using movement and instructing it gains an important meaning. Playing, experimenting, doing creative movements, physically expressing oneself with the body, exercising cooperation and communicating are all aspects, which can be experienced in the element of water. These experiences can be realized in all phases:

➤ Beginners' swimming.
➤ Advanced swimming.
➤ In various swimming sports.

This rough division into three content areas is covered in the three volumes of the "Aquafun" series. In Volume 1, the first steps with an emphasis on the 'little games' were covered. Volume 2, with the title "Games and Fun for the Advanced" devoted itself to the various games with a ball in water and how they are methodically structured.

This book aims to introduce creative playing and training playfully in the various swimming sports: underwater diving, artistic and high board diving, games with a ball, life saving, artistic and synchronized swimming, fitness in water and swimming training.

'Little Games'

The features of 'little games'
Before we introduce the 'little games' for the various areas of exercises for swimming, it is necessary to explain what is meant by **'little games'.**

Little Games are often differentially compared to the 'big games' (soccer, handball, field hockey, water polo etc.). With this in mind, each of them is designed to serve a particular purpose, which categorizes them according to function and they are characterized as methodical sequences compared to the 'big games'. They do not only have the function of leading up to the 'big games', they also have their own value, methods and aims.

After the statements above concerning the basic meaning of playing, this Chapter will cover the features of the 'little games' and then cover the various aims, in which little games can be used in sports instruction and in leisure and popular sports as well as competitive sports.

Little games have the following features, whereby in the list the word *little* is particularly emphasized:

Little people
Even very young children in pre-school age can be brought to follow various aims by using little games:
➤ Games designed to get the children, even one year-olds, to experience their body and to come to terms with what they can do and that they are able to carry out activities with their bodies, learning about space and time.
➤ By using games that require equipment, children learn to get used to equipment and personal things in their environment and put them into context and adequately put them to use.
➤ Games with the aim of experiencing social cooperation allow the children to develop social togetherness in small and large groups (c.f., above all the aims of motor pedagogy/motor psychology).
Of course little games can also be played by youths, grown-ups and other target groups such as older people, families etc.

Little groups

Little games can be played in small groups. Besides this there is often no set size of group like in the big games where the number of players is laid down. The size of the group can be flexible, so that large numbers of people can play all together in groups.

Little playing areas

Similarly the size of the playing area for little games is not laid down. Thus small groups can play in small areas. The larger the group, the larger the playing area has to be. The playing area should be adapted to take the size of the group playing on it.

Little rules

There is no international set book of rules. The description of the game can be quite short. Often the basic game idea of a little game can be expressed in one sentence. No rulebook is necessary like in the big games. Thus, little games can be played without a referee or game structures etc.

Variable rules

The rules of the game in little games can be adapted to suit the situation. Rule changes can come up because of external circumstances (location, equipment etc.,) or pedagogic reasons. Thus, for example, relay races can be organized so that children of different abilities e.g., disabled children, wheelchair-ridden children or overweight children may use a shorter turn-round point so that they have an equal chance to be able to take part.

No general competition rules

Because the rules are simple to follow and easier to manage, a nationally or internationally recognized set of competition rules is not necessary.

No or hardly any technical experience required

Little games can be played without technical prerequisites being necessary. While volleyball only functions when the participants are able to master the basic rudiments, in little games play takes place without having experience of any certain techniques. The children often learn adequate techniques, which they pick up as they play, so that the game functions even better.

No or only limited technical experience required
Little games are played without the requirement for any particular tactical knowledge. However, just as with sports techniques, basic tactics can be learned by using little games.

Little equipment
The requirement for equipment for little games is very small. One can play them without the need for a lot of equipment or at least only a little. There is no requirement for specialized equipment. Games of hitting a target can be played by using a basketball, tennis ball, medicine ball or even stones or snowballs.

No organizational requirements
The requirements to put a little game together are very minor. Therefore, little games can be played quite spontaneously.

No official game organization
Little games can be run without the organization required by the big games.

No national or international matches
In little games there are no heats or rounds and categories such as county or national tables etc, so therefore there are no national or international competition matches.

Fun & Joy
One of the most outstanding features of little games is the fun and joy one has when playing them. The games must be fun and encourage participants to enjoy moving about.

Reasons for and Uses of Little Games
The little games are divided into categories according to the various reasons and aims. They are very often used for certain pedagogic situations and these will have educational aims. They will also have a value on their own.

Little games can be used in sport and swimming instruction at every stage either in the introduction (warm-up), the main part or the conclusion of the session (cooling off).

In addition, they can be used on school playgrounds outside the sports instruction sessions, for example in school breaks or just for leisure.

➤ The pedagogic reason for little games

- Little games all have a purpose and value of their own. Little children play around freely without having a particular aim. In this sense one can speak of free play. Children try out games equipment and materials and see what they can do with them.
- Many little games have their own appeal and can be used not only for a particular purpose, but also as a game leading to one of the big sports games. So that the value of the game is properly felt, play should go on long enough and the actual value of the game should also be accentuated.
- One important task of the school institution is quite naturally **to teach games and play**. Young persons have to learn how to develop their personal and social abilities.
- **Using games in education** means matching the deliberate use of games in basic pedagogic situations. For this the games are given a function. They must fulfill a particular purpose and reach a specific aim. Correspondingly, the little games are used for particular pedagogical situations.

➤ The aims and uses of little games

- Making preparations for the big sports games:
  In many games books, little games play an important role by leading on to the big sports games: In this way games of throwing at targets can precursor basketball, games of catching and throwing lead to football or water polo and little diving games lead to underwater water polo etc.
- Fitness improvement:
  With the aim of improving fitness, little games gain an additional function. In this connection, little games are designed to train stamina, strength, speed, ability to coordinate, dexterity and agility inter alia for the big sports games.

- Social teaching:
  Little games can be used in sports instruction to further the teaching of social behavior. Using games, children learn to play together and accept the integration of persons with differing abilities as well as to communicate verbally and non-verbally.

➤ The use of little games in sports instruction
Little games can be used in every phase of sports or swimming instruction:

- **Introduction (Warm-up):** In the introductory part of the sports session, little games can serve to cover a playful warm-up period. In particular, movement intensive games, such as running and tagging games and little ball games, fulfill this task of warming up the body well.
- Little games, however, also lead up to the subject of the instruction, insofar that they can prepare the class for the main emphasis of that instruction.
- **Main Part:** Little games can serve to provide variety or provide a particular emphasis in the main part of a sports or swimming training session. For example they can fulfill the following educational aims by using games: social togetherness, cooperation, communication etc.
- The aims of motor system training can also be achieved by using little games: Games of catching and throwing teach the techniques involved in these actions, dribbling games, goal shooting games, jumping games etc., all prepare the student for learning the appropriate techniques in a playful manner.
- Little games can also be used to train for stamina, strengthening exercises, speed exercises, coordination abilities, agility and dexterity.
- **Conclusion (Cooling-off):** Little games are often used at the end of a session so that a playful end or an emotional highpoint is reached.

➤ The use of little games outside sports instructional periods
In daily school routine, little games have an important role also outside the sports instruction. The following categories of games can also be found outside sports instruction:

- Games to play during school breaks
- Playground games
- Field sports games
- Social games
- Role playing

➤ Games outside school time
Many of the little games can be used outside school time for festive or social occasions such as class outings, farewell parties inter alia. To go into detail about this would take us well out of the limits of what this book is about. Therefore, for now, here are a few examples:

- Festive games:
Group games such as "The hen and the fox"
(see RHEKER 2005, p 64) and dancing games.
- Games on a walking trip:
Country walks, "ABC Hike" (RHEKER 2000, pp 183/184)
and orienteering games etc.
- Class outings, Excursions:
Following on from excursions and class outings, colorful evenings can be arranged around themes. The participants can dress up to match the theme and they can decorate the room with bunting. Games can be put together to make a memorable evening. A game idea for a colorful evening after a diving excursion is included in Volume 2 (see RHEKER 2005, pp 105 'Diving Course Olympics').

1.4.2 'Big Games' with a Ball in Water

Various didactic concepts, which lead up to games with a ball in water, were covered in Volume 2. At this juncture, we will only cover a short overview of the game sequences connected with such games:

From the large palette of games with a ball in water, we will cover, first of all, the *little games* (games of catching, throwing and aiming with the ball), which serve as the basis for the big games. We build up on this with games and game sequences, which lead on to the big games of *water polo, water basketball and water biathlon*.

Further game sequences lead up to the following games with a ball in water: *Water volleyball* and *water soccer.* Using little games of diving underwater the game sequence for underwater polo is developed.

Furthermore, new games with a ball in water, which up to now are only rarely played or are not known - for example 'Aqua baseball' - will be covered (see RHEKER 2005).

Games for the Sport of Swimming   **1.4.3**

Games can liven up the running of training sessions in the various types of sport and give them a new accent:

> Running games in athletics.
> Games of strength and games of agility in strength events.
> Games in water in the various different areas of swimming sports (see Chapters 2.1 - 2.7).

As there is a lot of training necessary in the areas of swimming sports and the training methods are often monotonous and tiring, it makes it interesting to introduce playful forms of training into these sports areas.

The following areas of swimming sports should be included as playful games for this:

> Diving underwater
> Artistic and high board diving
> Life saving
> Artistic and synchronized swimming
> Fitness in water
> Swimming

Besides livening up things, these games and their forms are just as useful when learning to do techniques. This is demonstrated well by using the example of the various methodical ways of "Learning to do the Butterfly Stroke" (see Chapter 3).

1.4.4 Recursive: Pedagogical Basics –
Didactical Results – Methodical Application

In order to go over the main points of what has been covered so far, prior to going into the concrete elements of the exercises, and in the interests of brevity, we wish to mention the interdependence between pedagogic basic knowledge, didactic consequences and the approach to the general methodical processes, which form prerequisites for the step by step improvement of perfection. The environment of water can be made real through a variety of pedagogical aspects. In order to do justice to this variability, swimming instruction must not orient itself solely on teaching the techniques of swimming.

Concentrating only on some of the few techniques (the four Olympic swimming styles) results in the variety of being able to move in, by, on and under water becoming limited. This means that the development progress of the children will not be fully used.

Against this, situations with simple, freely constructed instruction enable more possibility to do movements.

In the following sections, both methods for the environment of water will be compared.

By deliberately turning away from the one-sided teaching of merely the techniques, some authors make a plea for a type of swimming instruction "oriented on experience (learning by doing)" (HILDEBRANDT 1999, p 248).

Because even beginners' swimming, which allows, first of all, for the basic possibility of "moving about in water" to be experienced, often the aim is to bring the beginners on as fast as possible to learn the sporting swimming techniques. Such early concentration on one or two swimming techniques alone limits the variety of movement in, by, on and under water. Furthermore, the possibilities of allowing the various abilities of the children in the environment of water to be developed are not considered.

"For the grounding of functional movement activities, for the development of the diverse perceptive faculty and activity sense and for being able to gain experience in moving about and the development of a feel for movement" (LOIBL 1992, p 31), an early orientation to movement activities such as swimming techniques is more likely to hinder than help.

A holistic pedagogical approach has the following aim:
The main thing is the *development of the whole personality* of the individual. Getting *to experience a whole host of movement experiences* takes priority over a one-sided learning of techniques. Having *fun by moving, playing games and sport* front up the situation. Priority targets are the learning processes of *independence, intrinsic motivation and a life-long, healthy sporting way of life, just as much as an active interconnection with the environment* (material experience).

In the area of beginners' swimming, this type of pedagogic approach is important. Particularly, playing and moving around in water offers the opportunity to be able to experience the various movements. They also offer the opportunity to try out and create one's own ability to move and to be part of constructing the content of the lesson and the educational lead-up to learning to swim.

Freely structured movement activities or prearranged instructional situations can be used to achieve these targets for all parts of beginners' swimming.

The educational task of a school and any other institution that delivers swimming instruction, such as swimming clubs, life saving societies etc., should therefore not concentrate primarily on the teaching of merely a few standard swimming techniques. On the contrary, the development of the whole of the personality should stand in the forefront, and with it, a varied training should be striven for. One which is not connected to one type of sport, but one which aims at the schooling of the coordination abilities and the full sense of perception.

"The aim of any exercising and training session is not only to improve a sporting technique or to learn coordination, but always to improve the ability of the individual's motor system". (HIRTZ 1994, p 117).

In order to give justice to this type of learning to swim, an adjustment of the methods should be made not only for beginners' swimming instruction. This is one, which turns away from a one-sided learning of techniques and gives more emphasis to a varied type of learning process, which is oriented towards experiencing things thus making it easier for the schooling of the individual senses and perceptive abilities. Swimming instruction should become something, which accompanies to build experiences and subjective aims about the element of water (c.f., HILDEBRANDT 1999, p 249).

In learning to swim, we are confronted with a process of learning to perceive the element of water and its various characteristics by the person. HILDEBRANDT (1999, p 251) calls this a "dialogue of every individual with the element of water". These experiences, which the children can have with and in water, are varied. They depend on the child's background and its previous experiences. These experiences that they can have with water are as varied as the children themselves. Free instruction should build on these varied experiences. It is also possible to integrate children with different abilities i.e., also children with disabilities and those without. This is because instruction, which is generally integrative, will contain more experience situations. "Learning, which is oriented on experiencing things, has the aim of connecting the independent and automatic actions of the person learning with his material and social environment" (HILDEBRANDT 1999, p 250). The learning process in swimming occurs automatically in conjunction with the element of water by playing and experimenting with games and becoming conscious of these experiences.

Instructional concepts, which are freely constructed and are not one-sided make possible methodical ways both to learn techniques and at the same time experience movement.

It's not a question of 'either - or' but rather more a question of 'as well as'.

When situations are created, in which children can have basic experiences in the environment of water, the exercises can be chosen so that these experiences with aims such as 'moving forward in water' can be sorted into themes. Moving on from there, one is lead to experimentation and choosing solutions for learning 'to swim like a fish'.

For the didactic production as a "dialogue of the factual problem" (LAGING 1999, p 2), in learning to swim the following movement activities can be used:
➤ Moving forward in water.
➤ Not sinking in water.

➤ Sinking in water.
➤ Moving underwater.
➤ Jumping into water.
➤ Playing with a ball in water etc.

When such freely chosen movement exercises are properly used in accordance with the aims, they will lead to experiencing movement, and they will be the basis for learning to swim.

Thus, general movement experiences such as moving forward in water, for example, can lead one to think about how to use the arms and hands when walking through the water, to trying out new ways of moving and to varying ways one knows. In connection with these varied experiences of movement, the coordination ability will be developed, which lead even to thinking about alternate and synchronized strokes (see RHEKER 1999a, pp 204-209).

In summary at this juncture, we can go into the arguments between learning to move using freely constructed movement exercises and learning to learn using a technically oriented basis.

The learning situation in sports and swimming instruction, where the students take part using freely constructed movement exercises in the element of water, is general and **freely constructed**. By comparison, sports instruction that is based on one-sided learning and predetermined techniques is called **formal instruction**.

In freely constructed sports instruction, many suggested solutions are possible and can be tried out. The children can be creative and come up with their own ideas. This will make it easier to experience many different ways of moving. In the formal, one-sided learning of techniques, the children stay more merely on 'receive', where they copy the techniques as laid down or as demonstrated by the instructor.

In this method, one orients oneself to the correct technique, shown in the textbooks as the ideal. By sticking to the traditional techniques, the students can be seen as being reproductive. By developing their own solutions in freely constructed instruction, they can use their own wit and even come up with new techniques. The method of finding one's own way and the use of individual techniques is particularly important for instruction of children who have experience of doing varied movements (c.f., New Concepts of Sports Instruction: BALSTER 1998, 1999, 2000 inter alia).

In freely constructed instruction children can come up with ways of moving on their own. In this way they are helped on to show their independence. Children also learn, at the same time, how to judge themselves and their ability to move. The children can work at doing this themselves. Assessments by third parties and a classification of performance in the formal instruction concept have to be compared against this argument.

Table 1: *Freely Constructed Movement Exercises – Learning Movements by Using Technical Methods*

Freely Constructed Movement Exercises	Learning Movements by Using Technical Methods
Freely constructed instructional situations	Formal Instruction
Many ways of doing things	Only one technique
Creativity	On receive
Varied movement experiences	One-sided learning of techniques
Be able to judge oneself	Third Party assessments
Finding out ways by oneself, Independence	No inducement to being independent
New techniques	Conventional techniques
Individual techniques	Traditional techniques
Understanding one's own movements	Extraneous understanding of movement
Varied learning prerequisites	Equal learning prerequisites
Individual speed of learning	Standardized speed of learning
Individual learning level	Standardized learning level
Learning about being social	Classification system
Impulse for the further development of the individual	Single-track
Process system	Oriented towards results
Productive	Reproductive
Centered around making experiences	Oriented towards results

Intrinsic motivation	Outside motivation
Having fun at moving, games and sports	
Basis for a lifelong, healthy, sporting life style	Learning the correct technique

Learning by using a system of freely constructed exercises is oriented towards making experiences and going through processes. Children with heterogeneous experience simply play together and do sport, because their individual, varied learning prerequisites have been taken into consideration when constructing the freely oriented systems. Everyone can play at his own particular level, occupy himself and come to terms with new movement experiences. In this way, an impulse for the further development of the individual is given. The various speeds of learning can also be taken into consideration.

With a system of formally learning movements by using a technical method, all the students are lead down a single-tracked route, *in-step* with each other (methodical sequence of exercises) to learn a single technique. This type of learning process is more or less oriented towards results.

In a system using movement exercises, children, of differing levels, can have a variety of experiences, which they share amongst themselves. This way they can learn from each other. Learning about social behavior, thus, gains its own valued place in the tuition.

By the sense of achievement, gained through a freely constructed instruction, children can have fun in moving, games and sport and are motivated to go on and learn more. They do not have to be motivated extraneously any more - they become intrinsically motivated. This can be the basis for a lifelong, healthy, sporting life style.

Along these lines, this is why freely constructed movement exercises will be found at the beginning of the following exercise chapters of this book for all areas of swimming sports. Additional games are included, which can be used not only as encouragement for further freely constructed tasks, but also represent ready-to-use game suggestions which can be played.

1.5 Swimming as an Integrative Sport

"Many little people, in many places,
doing a lot of small things, will change the face of the world."

(verse from the Third World)

At this juncture, we wish to introduce several basic arguments for swimming as an integrative type of sport. At the same time we would wish to illustrate those areas of swimming that have a capability of being used as an integrative medium.

Swimming is seen as an ideal type of sport for disabled people by many authors (LORENZEN 1970; KOSEL 1981; INNENMOSER 1988). This is because they can move in water on their own.

While people with paraplegia and people who cannot walk properly have to rely on aids such as wheelchairs or crutches on dry land, they are able to move around on their own without outside help in water.

Swimming (playing and moving in water) is also a very suitable type of sport for integrating margin groups, which in our society still includes people with disabilities.

The following circumstances can be counted as areas where joint swimming activities can be carried out by disabled and non-disabled people alike:

Meeting on the same level

People with differing situations can meet on the same level when swimming and playing in water. Children and grown-ups, men and women, people with and without disabilities move about when swimming with their head on the surface of the water - all on one level. Tall people don't have to look down at shorter ones, wheelchair bound people don't have to look up at pedestrians - children and grown-ups!

It is not always possible to look or talk to each other while swimming and diving through the water and that is why it is a lot easier for everybody to play together there. There is then the chance that we will treat each other as equals, perhaps also without prejudice, and meet all on the same level, communicate with each other freely or get together for joint activities.

Picture 2: *Integrated swimming - Blowing bubbles together*

Floating makes movement in water easier

The particular characteristics of the element of water form a general framework that allows people with disabilities to feel unhindered. The floating sensation that the body feels in water permits people with severe disabilities such as tetraplegia or MS to be able to move easier and more on their own than on dry land. In water, one can experience the feeling of 'body lightness'. Because practically the whole body (98%-100%) is freed from the gravitational pull by the floating effect, people, who can only move slowly or with difficulty on dry land, can now move about almost weightlessly and no longer feel restricted compared to people without disabilities. This is a matter of people who have disabilities such as damaged joints etc., but it also applies to people who are overweight or have other handicaps.

Learning to swim on equal terms

The area of beginners' swimming is particularly suitable for integrative experiences. In a group of beginner swimmers, they all start off with about equal conditions: No one can swim yet and everyone of them wants to or should learn to swim.

Therefore this is a good background for a group, consisting of disabled and non-disabled children to make their first experiences by using games in the water. On this basis, the elementary experiences of learning to swim can be done using further games and forms of exercises. Thus, children, with and without a disability, have similar beginners' conditions that permit them to be able to get to know jointly how to learn to swim. Because beginners' swimming instruction for non-disabled children starts off also with lots of little games, designed to let them get used to the water, there will also be no problem for the disabled ones to integrate and be able to join in. Particularly suitable games for these aims are interactive and communicative games.

Integration - Early on

Integrated sport, as a form of joint sport for disabled and non-disabled children, should be started as early as possible. Because prejudices manifest themselves, for example against margin groups, early on amongst, in particular the 4 to 8 year olds, children should be given the opportunity to play with disabled children in their pre-school years. In this way children learn to see them as people without prejudice and where the disability doesn't stand in the forefront of their thoughts.

Because beginners' swimming, already in pre-school age, shows good results, many groups work together on an integrated basis from the beginning. As a result, children with disabilities are not excluded at all from the beginning and non-disabled children get to mix with them without any form of prejudices.

Integration in leisure sports

Swimming, as a leisure and adventure sport, offers lots of opportunities to integrate people. It is easier to integrate different forms of disabled people in a form of sport that doesn't particularly depend on performance and success. In a sport that demands performance results from the people, those who don't possess this are quickly sidelined. A sport that bases itself on the motto of "Games and Sports for Everyone", on the other hand, permits those with very different conditions and situations to be able to take part - the young and old alike, disabled and non-disabled, top-performers and those with less ability.

Integration in other areas of swimming sports

Swimming is suitable, in all its facets, for the integration of margin groups, in particular for those people with a disability. Integration can be effected in all areas of the sport of swimming:

Beginners' swimming is particularly suitable (see above and RHEKER 2004 "Aquafun - First Steps").

Swimming as an aspect of leisure sport and recuperation

Vacation is just the time where people with different conditions and situations can be integrated in various activities at the seaside or other holiday locations using water activities.

Swimming and bathing in open-air and indoor swimming pools

Swimming and bathing in open-air and indoor swimming pools as well as in adventure pools, by lakes and at the seaside, can be used to integrate different target groups. These spacious facilities for activities and meeting up offer experiences and a form of leisure pursuit for everyone without exception. The rich palette of different activities on offer, which are clearly available in this type of activity facility, make it possible for disabled and non-disabled people to carry out integrated activities together alongside each other.

"Aqua Fitness"

The whole spectrum and availability of the area of "Aqua Fitness" can be quite fitting for the various target groups. Because practically all types of people with different conditions and situations can be brought together at the same time, "Aqua Fitness" is also an excellent medium to integrate people with a disability. This is the case in all aspects of "Aqua Fitness".

➤ Aqua Gymnastics

Water gymnastics can be done with many various aims and aspects so that heterogeneous groups can work out together. Water gymnastics can be done with and without equipment. Most of the aims for water gymnastics center on exercises for one's flexibility and the schooling of the ability to coordinate the body. Besides wanting to improve general stamina, the main aim of water gymnastics is to achieve a generally good degree of fitness. Because aims such as these cover all of the different types of people, the integration of disabled people is also quite possible.

➤ "Aqua Jogging"
Because "Aqua Jogging" is used for recuperative purposes, it is particularly suitable for the rehabilitation of the physically disabled as well as overweight and older people. It can also be used in health sports, leisure sports and serious sports. By virtue of the way that the joints are relaxed, older people with knee problems, people with a physical disability and non-disabled people can all train together.

➤ "Aquarobics"/"Aqua-Aerobics"
"Aquarobics" means the whole sphere of moving to music in water where it is used with the aim of improving fitness and the coordination abilities such as stamina, strength, coordination etc. With this aim, it is clear that people with quite different conditions and situations can do activities jointly together.

➤ "Aqua Wellness"
This new way of keeping fit aims at furthering a feeling of well being in water and the relaxation of tensions. Relieving tension is an important factor for many target groups, particularly for older people and people with problems and disabilities. Therefore, this aspect has a special value for the integration of people with different problems and situations.

Life Saving
Life saving emphasizes, in a special way, the social aim of being there for others. Therefore, disabled people can also be integrated into this aspect.
This should begin right from the teaching of beginners' swimming. Many life saving societies make this an important point in their work. However, the areas of getting out of trouble by oneself (saving yourself) and the games and training for saving others are also suitable for the integration of disabled persons.

Games with a ball in water
Games with a ball in water, particularly variations of those that lead on to competitive sports, can be played jointly by people with different abilities. Especially the area of swimming and playing in

water offers the possibility, not only of being active recuperatively and therapeutically, but also to be able to achieve the following aims:
➤ Having fun moving about.
➤ Playing together with others and building up social contacts.
➤ Developing new ways of moving and being creative.
➤ Being independent and being able to act on one's own.
➤ Being able to recognize one's own performance and improve it.
➤ Getting to understand the value of following a worthwhile leisure pursuit.

Underwater Diving

Underwater diving is a sport, which is also opening up more and more to disabled people (c.f., RHEKER 1997; HOFFMAN & others 1998). With a little openness and a lot of understanding lots of disabled people can participate in this attractive leisure activity. The fact that sometimes there is swapping over of roles *disabled - non-disabled,* can be seen in the example of diving with deaf people. While people with deafness disabilities can 'talk' to each other underwater using sign language, it is the able-bodied who don't understand and who can only help themselves with the few signs of the diving language.

Particularly the area of *health and stamina swimming* is suitable for people of different conditions and situations.

Swimming as a competitive sport

As a competitive sport, swimming does not have to be organized so that disabled people cannot participate. A good example of integration also in this area is the several times gold medal winner of the Paralympics, the German Britta SIEGERS, who trains alongside non-disabled athletes in the Cologne swimming club. The Paralympics in Sydney in 2000 showed that the nations, where the disabled athletes trained together with the non-disabled top athletes in competitive sports, they had the best chances of winning a medal.

All areas of swimming are suitable for the *rehabilitation and the maintenance of good health* in disabled persons, by virtue of the physical characteristics of water.

At the same time, they also give a good opportunity for joint activity, which furthers social integration in sport and eventually beyond that.

A decisive argument to support the integration of disabled persons by using sport lies in the social job of the educational institutes such as Kindergartens, schools etc. As an example, in Germany, many of the states have followed the model of Berlin and have begun to make it possible for disabled children, in any form, to attend normal schools.

These efforts at integration, naturally have not only repercussions on the institute of the school, but also on the training of sports teachers and their further training: Integration in education and *integration in sport must be mandatory subjects in the teacher training including the advanced levels.*

Besides the above arguments regarding content for integrated swimming instruction, at least for schools, there are also institutional ones.

The trainer's education should make the area of games and sports with disabled people and the integrative sports a subject of discussion.

The subject of integrated sports and swimming instruction is well covered in other places. These also show that many sporting applications can be transferred across from one to the other (see RHEKER 1995; 1996a/b; 1999b/c; 2000; 2004 and 2005). The basis of a concept for integration in swimming is the exercise oriented method of a "varied educational integration in sport for people of various conditions and situations" (see RHEKER 1999b; pp 179-195)

2 Impulses for Creative and Playful Training in the Sport of Swimming

"Even the smallest spring gets its water as a gift."

(Mara Joswich)

For many children, swimming is the most popular type of sport, because the environment of water to move in offers various possibilities to play in, by and under water. These different ways of experiencing things open up an intensive meeting with the element of water. Particularly the area of beginners' swimming often includes lots of games and a variety of different ways to move – see Volume 1 (RHEKER 2004 "Aquafun - First Steps"). Very often afer beginners' swimming, that is to say when one can swim properly, one only swims and exercises in straight lines (so to speak counting the tiles). As reviews and studies have proved (BRETTSCHNEIDER/BRÄUTIGAM 1990; RHEKER 1996c), this leads to a clear drop in popularity amongst older children.

Contrary to this, there are many possibilities to be creative and varied in the environment of water after learning to swim. The variable game forms, particularly the 'little games', which lead on to the 'bigger games' in water (water polo, water basketball, underwater ball, water volleyball, water biathlon etc.,) were presented in Volume 2 (RHEKER 2005 "Aquafun - Games and Fun for the Advanced").

This chapter aims at showing that, besides games with a ball in water, there are other areas of the sport of swimming that can be enriched with a variety of games and game forms.

It will not only cover how to construct playful training forms for swimming exercises, it will also bring in training for the other areas of artistic and high diving, life saving, artistic and synchronized swimming, water fitness and underwater diving.

The fact that the area of learning techniques can also be covered by games can be seen in the example of the introduction of butterfly swimming by using playful means (see Chapter 3).

By constructing the areas of swimming sports in a playful manner one refers back to the pedagogic aspects (KURZ 2000), which speak of a free understanding of sport. This is why activities from the area of swimming can be given a purpose in different ways.

The area of *'Aqua Fitness',* which is primarily associated with the purpose of *health*, can be linked together with the following pedagogic aspects:

Furthering one's health, developing a health consciousness
Using this aspect of doing something for one's health and fitness, Aqua Fitness is done mainly using several offshoots: 'Aqua Jogging', Water gymnastics, "Aqua Wellness" etc.

Improving one's perception, broadening one's experience of moving
In Aqua Fitness new sequences of movement can be learned. Learning about one's own body and the possible ways of moving it can be experienced afresh.

Expressing oneself using the body, making movements
The ability to express oneself using the body can be developed particularly by playing and doing exercises to music. Individuals or groups can do the movements alone or together.

Trying out things on one's own and being responsible
When one is doing jogging in deep water and when one is driving oneself to one's own limits, this means that will-power and daring are being shown as well as learning about being able to judge oneself.

Experiencing one's capability, understanding it and being able to judge it
When doing a good workout of water gymnastics, which is matched to one's individual limits, one can learn very quickly how to judge one's ability and assess it.

Cooperating, being competitive and communicating
These aspects come into being in partner and group activities as well as in the play periods.

In a similar way, the other areas of swimming can be seen as having the same aspects of purpose. So that the exercises in the instruction for the various areas of swimming can be managed using the various pedagogic aspects, at the beginning of each chapter of exercises, several examples of approaching this in each area are suggested.

Using freely constructed movement exercises or instruction with projects, new ways of approaching the environment of water can be opened up:

Freely constructed situations in the instruction create opportunities that encourage experimentation and tests and these produce various ways of getting round movement problems. Finding out the various ways by themselves forces the children to judge their own capabilities and have confidence in them.

Important impulses are given for the further development of the individual. Each can play, work and find out things at his own individual level.

In instruction freely arranged like this, young persons can become creative and develop their own ideas. This encourages them to have fun at moving and playing games and sports and at the same time they provide a basis for a lifelong, healthy sporting activity.

Swimming instruction, based on learning experiences such as these, gives the opportunity for a variety of lessons to be learned in the environment of water. All methods of moving about can be tried out: Movements carried out using the following exercises make for easier learning:

- What can I do so that I don't sink in water?
- How can I move forward in water with and without touching the bottom (see RHEKER 2004 (Aquafun - First Steps), pp 185-200)?
- How can I stay underwater for a while?
- How can I stay longer underwater?
- What do I have to do in order to move about underwater?
- How can I get into the water?
- How can I swim easier (not so easy)?

Impulses for Creative and Playful Diving

2.1

"If you jump into the water,
then act like a fish."

Herbert OTTO

Introduction

2.1.1

Swimming instruction that fulfills its various pedagogic aims has to be designed to be multi-aspect. Swimming instruction that covers a variety of purposes comes over well with all pupils and leads many different people on to live an intensively active life.

The activities that we do in the environment of water can be given a purpose in various different ways. This is very much the case in the sport of swimming as well as in underwater diving. Underwater diving can have the following pedagogic aspects:

Trying out things on one's own and being responsible
From the first attempts of putting the head in water, up through to swimming underwater and diving down deep, will-power and daring are demanded. When snorkeling and when diving with compressed air bottles, you have, at the same time, an important responsibility towards your partner. The partner and the impressive underwater world should be watched continuously.

Improving one's perception, broadening one's experience of moving
When diving underwater, the perception of one's own body can be experienced afresh and extended by the fact that the floating sensation and movements can be felt in three dimensions, on the surface and underwater. The ways of moving the body are broadened continuously by learning new movements such as submerging, swimming along underwater and diving with a snorkel or compressed air etc.

Expressing oneself using the body, making movements
Underwater, movements can be made which are very expressive and creative.

Experiencing one's capability, understanding it and being able to judge it

After having completed a stretch swimming underwater or a slalom course, one can judge one's own performance and judge it just as well as having completed a successful session of underwater polo.

Cooperating, being competitive and communicating

Cooperation and communication are absolutely essential when diving underwater with equipment and when doing many game forms of diving underwater. Diving gives us the knowledge of a new kind of communication. These aspects, regarding the purpose of comparison and winning/losing, can be seen also in competition situations such as in underwater polo.

Furthering one's health, developing a health consciousness

In order to develop health consciousness, one has to be aware of the dangers and risks of diving and be able to judge these correctly. However, one can also enjoy the positive side of diving and these will contribute to a healthy outlook on life.

So that the exercises for this element of swimming - diving - occur under the aegis of the various pedagogic aspects, you will find several examples of the free approach to the subject at the beginning of the chapter.

When swimming sessions are conducted with a particular theme as center point, these are called game projects. Examples are given.

Simple diving games from the area of beginners' swimming that were included in part in Volume 1 "Aquafun - First Steps" (RHEKER 2004) follow. In order to avoid repetition, the diving games, relevant to this chapter, will only be mentioned by name or various games will be put together according to category.

At the beginning are games that have moving underwater as a theme. They begin with simple games using safe and controlled movements underwater in the beginner's pool and lead up to diving games for snorkeling in the main pool. Following on from games with flippers, diving mask and the snorkel, several games are suggested, which can be done with compressed air bottles.

The following diving games can be used for various aims in the swimming lesson inter alia:

> Diving games are an important element of the swimming instruction, because they can bring in new dimensions of moving in water and enliven the swimming instruction.
> They can be used to target the learning and schooling of the aim of the project, namely being able to move about underwater.
> They are best suitable to improve orientation underwater with and without use of the snorkel equipment.
> They prepare one for diving and snorkeling in open waters.
> The games in the last chapter are suitable for the playful employment and training of diving with equipment.

Before carrying out the first diving games in the swimming pool, the pupils should get some information about the physical peculiarities of diving (for this see also Volume 1 "Aquafun - First Steps" p 134 et seq).

> Equalizing the pressure - see Chapter 2.1.7.
> Hyperventilation, swimming pool "blackout" - see Chapter 2.1.7.
> Information on the diving goggles/mask - see Chapter 2.1.6.

Free forms of Movement in Diving 2.1.2

By using freely constructed movement exercises for diving, children (and grown-ups) can gather a lot of experience on how they can put their head in water, how they can submerge and swim a stretch underwater etc. In relation to these various basic experiences, playful forms of diving can be developed.

When putting the freely constructed movement exercises together, one should take care that they are made so that everyone is encouraged to do his own thing, and has sufficient time and space to experiment and try things out. Subsequently, the movement solutions that have been discovered are shown to the group so that other group members are encouraged to try other things out for themselves. The variety of movements achieved this way is always very large and can bring more stimuli to learning movements than any teacher could achieve sitting at his desk preparing the lesson. The children become more independent by trying things out for themselves. The personal initiative of discovering ways of moving develops the children's creativity and makes sure that they are highly motivated in participating in the lesson itself *(intrinsic motivation)*.

By using the following movement exercises, diving can be constructed in a playful and flexible manner:

Letting the body or parts of the body sink underwater

How can I let the body or parts of it sink underwater?
First of all, one tries out letting parts of the body sink and then goes on to letting the whole body sink.

Variations:

- Letting parts of the body sink in varying depths of water in the beginner's pool: waist-deep, chest-deep, shoulder-deep.
- In the main pool, letting parts of the body sink at various depths.
- In the main pool, letting the whole body sink at different depths.
- Letting the body sink with additional weights.

Floating

How can I let my body or parts of it float on water?
The children have to find out how they can let their body or parts of it float on the water.

Variations:

- In the beginners' pool let the body or parts of it float on the surface.
- In the main pool let the body float on the surface.
- In the main pool let the body float at different depths.
- Floating the body in water holding it in various different ways.
- Floating the body in water with different breathing methods.
- Let the parts of the body or the whole body float holding different equipment: Pull buoys, Aqua Jogging belt, balloons etc.
- As an exercise with a partner: In the main pool, both of the partners' bodies float at different depths.

Sinking fast

How can I make my body sink faster?
The children try out how they can make their body sink faster in water with and without the use of equipment. For this, lots of equipment is made available to experiment with.

Variations:
- In the main pool let the body sink in varied depths.
- Using additional equipment such as diving rings, hand weights etc., let parts of the body sink by holding them.
- Let the body sink in different depths at different speeds.
- Let the body sink in water, holding it in different ways: Vertically feet first, vertically headfirst, diagonally, slanting etc.
- Using weights as aids let the body sink.

Surfacing the body
How can I surface the body quicker?
The children try to find out how they can get their body to the surface with and without the use of equipment. For this, various pieces of equipment are made available.
Variations:
- In the main pool let the body surface from various different depths.
- Parts of the body are made to surface using equipment such as pull buoys, swimming boards, swimming rings, balloons etc.
- Let the body surface from different depths at different speeds using various equipment (see above).
- Let the body surface holding it in various different ways: vertically feet first, vertically headfirst, diagonally, slanting, lying on the stomach, lying on the back etc.

Moving forwards underwater
What ways are there to move forward under water?
See Chapter 2.4.4.

Communicating underwater
How can I communicate with my partner underwater?
While underwater diving try to send the partner a message.
Variations:
- Use underwater sign language to communicate with the partner.
- Tell your partner something by singing or speaking underwater.
- Submerge in the main pool, at different depths, and communicate with your partner using sign language.
- Tell your partner something by miming the message.
- Swim underwater for a stretch with your partner and converse in diver's sign language.

Prolonging your stay underwater

By experimenting, find out how you can prolong your stay underwater.

Variations:

- Prolong your stay underwater without any aids: Using breathing techniques, concentration, help from the partner etc.
- Prolong your stay underwater with aids: Snorkel, drinking straw, oxygen bottles, with buckets filled with air, mouth to mouth breathing with a partner etc.

Keeping the balance

How can one hold the body level at the same height while at different depths in the water?

Variations:

- In the beginner's pool, holding the body at different angles (squatting, sitting, lying on the stomach) at the same depth by using breathing techniques.
- In the main pool, keeping the body at the same height in different depths of water by using breathing techniques.
- Keeping the body at the same height in different depths of water by using the lead diver's belt and diving jacket for diving underwater with compressed air.

Rapid surfacing

How can one surface rapidly?

Various different types of equipment can be made available for this exercise.

Variations:

- In the main pool, surface from different depths by kicking off from the bottom and shooting up out of the water as far as possible.
- From different depths, surface at different speeds using additional equipment such as pull buoys, swimming boards, swimming rings, balloons etc.
- Surface with the body at different angles: feet first, headfirst, diagonally, slanting etc.
- Surface rapidly together with your partner.

Ice holes

In the main pool, several rings are laid floating on the surface to represent 'air holes'.

Who can submerge themselves and surface up through one of the air holes to breathe?

Picture 3: *Who can get the furthest in the water with dry feet?*

Keeping your feet dry

A group tries to get as many of its members to the other side of the pool without their feet getting wet.

Variations:

- Get your partner to the other side of the beginner's pool with his feet still dry.
- As many people as possible from the group get to the other side with their feet still dry.
- One of the groups builds a 'living' bridge with their bodies, over which the people get to the other side.
- In the main pool, as many people as possible from the group get to the other side with their feet still dry.
- In open waters: Which group can get a member of the side as far out as possible into the water with his feet still dry?

2.1.3 Game Projects

In instruction oriented towards doing projects, the swimming lessons can center round a specific theme (for a comprehensive explanation see RHEKER 2005, "Aquafun - Games and Fun for the Advanced" pp 97-106). Games and exercise forms are selected and put together for a theme framework, or the whole period can take the form of telling a story.

Project lessons like these can be stretched over several periods and can be held in cooperation with other disciplines (for example the subject of 'surfacing' can be done in conjunction with the physics teacher).

Project lessons for swimming can be constructed as follows:

Introduction to the theme:
1. Using a story.
2. Depicting a special situation.
3. Using a backdrop scene for playing with different equipment available.
4. Using annual events as themes such as Winter, Thanksgiving or Carnival.

Developing the project
From the introductory story, ideas can be developed on how the situation can be played and extended.

Points for the program can be worked out in work groups (teams) and brought together for the whole program.
   A play scene can be divided up into various stations and worked on by small groups with the idea of people visiting each station.

Project result/Finale
The results of the working groups are brought together and can be presented in a finale. The theme can also conclude with a climax.
After a longer project phase there is also the opportunity to present the results in a performance.

In projects to do with movement, all the participants should be given freedom to bring in their own ideas and imagination to the instruction. By virtue of the openness of the instruction in this situation, it often happens that the children can be very active. Anxious children can be very withdrawn and shy, but these will also have the opportunity to get involved without appearing stupid or fear making mistakes.

At this point in the chapter, we want to show an example of how such a project can appear. Using the theme of "Treasure Hunt" or the "Pirate Ship", games and exercises for the lesson on diving can be put into an exciting story. For this various pieces of equipment must be made available (swimming boards, swimming buoys, pool noodles, rubber rings and air-beds). These can be used to build the pirates' ship that is going to be loaded with 'treasures' (stones wrapped in aluminum kitchen foil paper, diving rings, cutlery, old coffee cans, children's toys etc) and put to sea. On the journey the ship and its crew will be subjected to various adventures:

The ship is caught in a storm. It tosses about wildly and the waves wash over the boat. Part of its load is lost overboard.
The storm increases until the ship capsizes and all the 'treasures' sink to the bottom of the sea (in the beginners' pool).
The daring pirates manage to rescue themselves on buoys and boards and reach the shore (edge of the pool). After the storm subsides, they now try to recover the 'treasure'. The first divers are sent off to do this. Diving teams can also be formed and these try to recover as many treasures as possible.

Jeux sans Frontières
Various stations can be set up, which possess a high challenge (see RHEKER 2005 "Aquafun - Games and Fun for the Advanced" pp 92/93).

Diving Games
From the area of diving games (see also Chapters 2.1.4 and 2.1.5), games can be put together to form a course. Further game projects can be found in "Aquafun - Games and Fun for the Advanced" pp 100/106 (RHEKER 2005).

2.1.4   Underwater Diving Games in the Beginners' Pool

At the beginning, diving games will be introduced that refer back to the partial aims of beginners' swimming. The first diving games from Volume 1 "Aquafun - First Steps" (RHEKER 2005) show the methodical sequence of how children learn to bring the head to touch water, then how they lay it on the water and then in the next step put it right under the water.

Orienting oneself underwater and the deliberate method of moving forward form the following aims that are done as game forms, first of all in shallow water and then, later, also in deeper water as they get more difficult.

Splashing water with the feet
The children sit on the edge of the pool with their feet dangling in the water. When a signal is given they kick around hard with their feet splashing.

(This game is very good as a warm-up game or to lead up in a playful manner to the foot actions for the crawl or the foot action with flippers).
Variations:
- Splashing with only one leg.
- Moving the legs with different force.
- Splashing with hands and feet.
- Splashing with the feet while lying on the stomach.
- Making the water 'boil'.
- Splashing wearing flippers.

Further Games (see Vol 1):
"Splashing the others until they are soaked", "Washing games", "Watering flowers", "Blowing a hole in the water", "Fireman's pump".

Games in a circle and singing games where water is sometimes splashed in the face:
"Eeny, Miny, Mo", "Ring-a-ring o' roses", "Up I stretch", "Show your feet".

Running and catching games where water is sometimes splashed in the face:
"What's the time Mr. Shark?" (especially the variation to frighten the shark away), "The sea calls all fish", "Duck hunting", "Fisherman, Fisherman - How deep is the water?"

Games where the children learn to lay their face on the water

Glass Bottomed Boat
A tire inner tube is laid on the water to represent the glass bottom. The children watch the 'fish' in the sea through the 'glass bottom' by laying their faces in the water.

Singing songs underwater
One of the children sings a simple song underwater. The others lay their heads on the water or dive down and try to guess the tune.

Further games
"Pushing the Water Polo Ball", "Diving along the Side of the Pool", "Submerging the Head - with Assistance", "Diving Down Underwater Round Objects", "Heading objects", "Fireman's pump" (see RHEKER, 2004 pp 136/137).

Games for orientation under water in the beginners' pool

Laying the face on water and opening the eyes
The children lay their faces on the water and open the eyes to orientate themselves. After they have oriented themselves while standing, they move through the water with their eyes open laying their faces on the water.

Retrieving objects out of the water
Various things (rubber rings, diving stones, treasures etc.,) are spread about on the bottom of the beginners' pool. The children have to retrieve them.
Variations:
- Retrieving objects (rubber rings, treasures etc.,) from different heights at the steps.

- Retrieving objects out of hip-deep water.
- Retrieving objects out of chest-deep water.
- Retrieving objects out of shoulder-deep water.
- Retrieving lots of objects with a partner.

Making figures underwater

Various objects are spread under water that they form figures. The children have to dive from one object to another to try to identify the figures.

Diving against the clock

The children dive and try to hold their breath for a length of time.
Variations:
- Partner Diving: A partner dives down and the other partner counts the time the other can stay underwater.
- Who can stay the longest underwater? A partner and an instructor keep watch to make sure no-one loses consciousness (swimming pool blackout).

Underwater caving

Two or three children are holding tire inner tubes, sticks or other obstacles one behind the other underwater. The children now try to dive through the formed 'caves'.
Variations:
- Five inner tubes are held in a row.
- The 'cave' twists and turns.
- At the end of the 'cave' is a 'treasure trove' that has to be retrieved.

Slalom diving

Several partners stand next to each other in a row so that their straddled legs form a slalom course. Each child dives through this course once.
Variations:
- Slalom diving as a relay.
- Slalom diving around underwater slalom poles.
- Diving through the straddled legs of several partners.
- Diving through a number of hoops being held up or through hoops on the ground.

Further Games
"Pulling faces", "Counting fingers", "Moving things underwater", "Flotsam and Jetsam", "Fire brigade pump", "Sinking", "Elevator", "Who can sit on the bottom of the pool?", "Pull and dive", "Merry-go-round", "Cat and Mouse", "Over and under", "Diving through the partner's straddled legs", "Diving in turns", "Diving a figure of eight", "Eel", "Diving through a hoop", "Tunnel-Diving", "Walking on the hands", "Retrieving objects from different depths of water" (see "Aquafun - First Steps" (RHEKER 2004, pp 138-145)).

Underwater Diving Games in the Main Pool

2.1.5

After the games for the basic situation of being able to control oneself underwater in the beginners' pool, in this chapter, first of all, we introduce simple diving games in the main pool. These can be used for leading up to diving with the snorkel.

Diving, breathing out
The children try to breathe out while diving and thereby let themselves sink to the bottom of the pool.
Variations:
• Diving down feet first.
• Diving down headfirst.

Who can dive the furthest?
All the children start from the long side of the pool.
They place their feet on the wall and push themselves off at a signal.

Take care!
When doing longer stretches, each diver must be individually monitored.
Variations:
• Diving a length.
• Diving underwater after diving in.
• Diving with flippers.

Diving down a slalom course

Diving through a slalom course of poles.

Variations:

- Doing the slalom course as a relay.
- Doing the slalom carrying an object.

Obstacle diving

Diving through a tube.

Variation:

The tube is never-ending because it is being moved along by two partners.

Picture 4: *Obstacle diving through a moving tube*

Diving in pairs

Two children stand opposite each other. Between them there is a diving ring in the water. At a signal both dive to get the ring. Whoever gets it first gives it to the partner, who places the ring back on the bottom of the pool.

Diving in Phases

Several diving rings are laid down a lane behind each other. Each diver dives for these rings in the following manner: At the first ring the diver expels some air, at the second one some more. By the time the fourth or fifth ring is reached all the air has been expelled and the diver has to surface.

Underwater Rendezvous

Two children dive in from opposite sides and try to meet each other underwater in the middle and then surface again together.

Variations:

- Before they surface they exchange underwater signs.
- Before they surface they exchange diving rings.
- Before they surface they dive around each other underwater.
- Before they surface they both do a roll underwater.

Water Giants

One of the children sits on the shoulders of another child. Which couple can get the furthest from shallow water into deeper water?

Diving Bell

A bucket, hanging from a 5kg diving ring, is sunk to the bottom of the pool. The relay team members now dive down one after the other and blow air into the bucket until it surfaces on its own

Never-ending Underwater Diving Relay

3-4 children are spread across the width of the pool. The first diver swims underwater to the next person carrying a ring, which he hands to the next one underwater. The next one repeats the exercise etc. Which group manages more than a length?

Variations:

- Which group dives underwater the longest distance?
- Which group can manage to do the obstacle course best?
- Which group stays underwater for the longest time?
- An underwater polo ball is carried while diving.

Adaptable diving

According to the number of players of a group, objects are distributed on the bottom at different distances from the edge of the pool.

Dependent on its capabilities, each child collects an object. Which group can collect all the objects first?

Treasure Diving Race

Two teams are formed and they line up on the longer edge of the pool. Various treasures are strewn around in the water (diving rings, underwater polo balls, diving stones etc. On a signal each team tries to collect as many treasures as they can. Which team has collected the most treasures?

Variations:

- Which team has collected the most treasures when each member is only allowed to collect one at time?
- Which team collects the most treasures when they do it as a relay?
- Four groups are formed and each starts from one corner of the pool.

"Buddy" Diving

Two partners swim and dive alternately. One of them dives first of all while the other one accompanies him on the surface. As soon as the diving partner surfaces the second one starts his dive.

Creative Diving

Who can dive underwater in the most individual creative manner? Who has the most imaginative diving technique?

Island Diving

2-3 tires are laid down on one of the lanes of the pool. Each diver now tries to dive a length underwater and can only resurface to breathe once he is in one of the tires.

Variations:

- The number of tire inner tubes can be reduced.
- Doing Island Diving as a relay race.
- Underway, one or two diving objects have to also be picked up.

The Guard Dog Game

Several different 'treasures' are lying on the bottom of the pool. A child or the instructor is guarding the 'treasures'. All the other children try to grab as many of them as possible. If a child is touched by the 'guard dog', he has to drop the 'treasure', swim back to the edge of the pool and begin again.

Singing Underwater
Diving down and singing songs underwater: Whoever guesses which tune is being sung, is the next to sing a song.

Blind Diving
One partner swims underwater for a certain, straight distance with closed eyes. The other partner goes along with him and leads him.
Variations:
- The 'blind' partner swims underwater through a slalom.
- The 'blind' partner swims underwater collecting 'treasures'.
- The 'blind' partner swims underwater wearing darkened goggles.

Further Games
"Diving and breathing out", "Changing rings", "Snakes", "Collecting colors", "Timed diving", "Sinking partners", "Lifting up the partner" (see RHEKER 2005, "Aquafun - Games and Fun for the Advanced" pp 134-153).

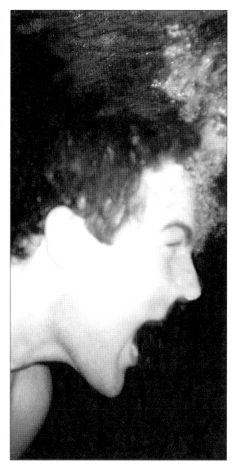

Picture 5: *Singing songs underwater is fun*

2.1.6   The Basics of Underwater Diving with Equipment

After having covered games in the previous chapter that represented **the basis of moving about in water,** this section deals with games especially for diving with snorkeling equipment. We not only show games that deal with the individual pieces of snorkeling equipment (flippers, mask and snorkel tube), but also how one can play with the whole equipment.

The games lead up to improved orientation underwater with the snorkeling equipment and prepare the diver for diving and snorkeling in open waters. At the same time, they provide a basis for games with a ball underwater.

For the methodical lead-up to diving with the snorkel equipment, the emphasis should not be laid on learning techniques and diving training. Rather more, it should work at learning to assimilate diving with the snorkel in a playful manner.

First of all, games and game forms will be introduced for swimming and diving with flippers. Games for use with the mask and the snorkel tube follow on from this and finally, games for the complete use of the snorkel equipment round the chapter off.

So that the games for snorkel diving can be played correctly, we include here some remarks about using the flippers, the mask and snorkel tube as an introduction.

Snorkel Equipment

Flippers: The flippers should have a closed foot compartment, which should fit the foot well. Between the foot compartment and the flipper blade there should be an angle of approximately 15 degrees. The hardness of the flippers themselves and their length is dependent on the ability of the swimmer.

Diving Mask: The mask should have the following features: They must have a nose valve, easily reachable, so that the pressure can be released without difficulty. The lens must be made of security glass. A double sealing band and soft material (silicon or rubber) must provide a good fit and seal well. An adjustable headband should be fixed by an adjuster at the center of the rear of the head so that the mask sits firmly. The field of view must be large and the mask volume small.

Snorkel: The snorkel tube should be no longer than 35 cms and have a diameter of 1,5 - 2,5 cms. The mouthpiece with the gum hold should be individually fitted to the size of the mouth. The upper extremity or the whole snorkel tube should have a noticeable color (see KROMP et al. 1996; STIBBE 1994).

Getting used to the Snorkel Equipment
Flippers

Before the children swim with flippers for the first time, they must receive some basic instruction on how to use them.

You should never walk around on dry land with flippers on. This is because there is a great danger of having an accident. You can easily fall over with them on. Walking around in them also damages them. The flippers therefore should be put on either sitting on the edge of the pool or in the water. You can slip into them much easier this way and it avoids having to walk in them.

When you swim with flippers, you are very fast, therefore to start with you should swim slowly and carefully. Swimming in flippers demands a lot of energy. As a result, for the inexperienced, you can get cramps in the calves easily.

Diving Mask

So that the glass in the mask does not cloud over, you rub some spittle on to the dry glass and rinse it out. The mask is put on so that it sits firmly without pressing. The volume of the mask should be small, so that the pressure can be regulated (released) quickly and easily when diving. If you cannot release the pressure with a diving mask when diving, you should not dive with one.

Exercises for getting used to the diving mask

- In the beginners' pool, put the mask on and lay the head on the water.
- Put the mask on in the beginners' pool and look around underwater.
- Put the mask on in the beginners' pool and look at another person and make contact with him.
- Swim with the diving mask with and without flippers.

- So that you can clear the mask and overcome the water/nose breathing reflex, you have to practice being able to breathe out through the nose underwater.
- Clearing the mask:
  In order to learn how to clear the diving mask, first of all, put the head underwater in the beginners' pool, flood the mask i.e., let water into the mask. Then you place your hand on the back of your neck, place the upper rim of the mask against the forehead and blow air into the mask through the nose. This blows the water out of the mask so that it is full of air again.

Snorkel:
With the snorkel you only breathe through the mouth, therefore this action has to be learned first of all in simplified situations before it can be used to dive and snorkel.
- Place the snorkel in the mouth and breathe through it on dry land.
- Place the snorkel in the mouth, lay the head on the water in the beginners' pool and breathe through it.
- Place the snorkel in the mouth, swim along on the surface of the water and breathe through the snorkel.
- Swim along with the snorkel and diving mask and breathe through the snorkel.

Clearing the snorkel tube
Put the diving mask on and take the snorkel in the mouth. In the beginners' pool put the head under the water. Water will flood into the snorkel tube. You now bring your head up straight and blow the water out through the tube using short, strong, explosive puffs.
Variation:
- Clear the snorkel tube when snorkeling or after diving under the water.

Snorkeling in waves
Snorkel along on the surface of the water and then dive underwater and swim along submerged for a few meters. After surfacing blow the snorkel tube clear and carry on snorkeling. After a short stretch repeat the exercise and so on.

Physical Peculiarities and Safety Measures when Underwater Diving

Regulating pressure

When diving, the pressure increases as you go deeper, so the diver has to regulate this pressure. When snorkeling, this pressure can be felt in the middle ear and in the diving mask. When submerging, you should continually regulate the pressure right from the beginning so that at no time the pressure is there.

To regulate the pressure (clear it) the Valsalva system is used where the nose is squeezed between the thumb and forefinger (nose window on the diving mask) and air is gently pressed into the area of the epiglottis. The pressure can also be released by swallowing hard or by pulling the lower jaw down.

Hyperventilation

If you are suffering from hyperventilation you should not swim underwater or dive.

With hyperventilation, you breathe in and out rapidly and continuously. This causes a drop in the CO_2 content of the blood, which is very necessary for controlling the breathing apparatus.

It can then happen that the need to breathe sets in later and the brain eventually lacks oxygen leading to the so-called swimming-pool-blackout. The diver loses consciousness underwater and breathes in water as the breathing function comes into action and there is a danger of drowning.

Observation by the partner

Underwater diving is a partner sport. One should never dive alone. Always dive with someone else or with some monitoring on the surface.

Observe the following golden rule: Never dive alone!

2.1.8 Games with Equipment for Underwater Diving

Games with Flippers
In order to get used to flippers, games can be chosen at the beginning, which tie in with well known techniques such as the leg stroke for the crawl. At the same time, by using these games and game forms, the movements of the legs for the crawl, backstroke and butterfly can be improved.

Leg stroke swimming with flippers
The leg stroke for the crawl is done wearing flippers - first of all swimming over short stretches and then, later, longer stretches.
Variations:
- The crawl leg stroke on the back.
- The crawl leg stroke underwater.
- Swimming the crawl leg stroke with one flipper.
- Coordination of the full crawl leg strokes.
- The crawl leg stroke with flippers done as a relay.
- The crawl leg stroke done swimming on one side.
- The butterfly leg stroke.

Swimming the crawl with flippers
The full crawl leg stroke is done wearing flippers.
Variations:
- Swimming a length on the stomach doing the crawl with flippers.
- Swimming a length on the back doing the crawl with flippers (backstroke crawl).
- Swimming several lengths using the crawl with flippers.
- Swimming a relay race using the crawl and flippers.

Putting the flippers on
The swimmer throws the flippers into the water and dives after them to put them on in the water.
Variations:
- Putting the flippers on underwater.
- Putting the flippers on underwater and diving a stretch underwater (e.g., 10 m).

As a relay race: Put the flippers on, swim a length underwater and pass the flippers on to a partner, who also puts them on underwater etc.

The Water High Jump

Balloons are suspended at different heights from a line over the pool. Who can touch the balloons at their different heights by doing a leg kick out of the water?

Variations:

- Who can touch the balloons with the head?
- Can the members of a group each touch a different balloon?
- Sweets are suspended over the pool at different heights. Who can pluck the sweets off the line by executing a leg kick out of the water?

Number Race with Flippers

2-4 teams each form circles. Each team member is allotted a number. On the bottom of the pool, a pair of flippers lies in the center of each circle. When the instructor calls out a number, the child with that number has to dive down, put on the flippers and swim round their circle.

Carrying Relay with Flippers

Objects are used as a baton in a relay.

Variations:

- A pull buoy is carried swimming forwards, backwards or sideways.
- Diving rings of different weights are carried.
- A pull buoy is carried so that it doesn't get wet.
- The pull buoy is carried underwater.
- Different distances are covered: One, two or three widths.
- Various different swimming techniques are used: Crawl, backstroke crawl, breaststroke or butterfly.

Flipper Diving

Several teams are formed, which dive in a relay race against each other. First of all the crawl leg stroke is used.

Variations:

- Diving using the crawl leg stroke lying on the stomach.
- Diving using the butterfly leg stroke lying on the stomach.
- Diving using the crawl leg stroke swimming on the side.
- Diving using the crawl leg stroke lying on the back.
- Diving using the butterfly leg stroke swimming on the side.
- Diving using the butterfly leg stroke lying on the back.

- Various distances are covered: One, two or three widths.
- Swimmers dive a length underwater.
- Diving through a slalom course.

Changing Direction, Swimming Wearing Flippers
Various objects (diving rings, stones, 'treasures' etc.,) are laid down anywhere on the bottom of the pool. The divers can now dive down, touch an object and then change direction towards another object to touch that one.

Copy-cat Diving
Two divers swim underwater after each other in line. The second one has to follow and copy all the movements and changes of direction made by the one in front.
Variations:
- The first swimmer thinks up all the different ways of moving forwards: Crawl leg kick on the stomach and on the back, butterfly leg kick and different arm actions with each stroke.
- Change directions at different intervals.
- Change also the swimming speed.
- The ways of moving forward, the direction as well as the swimming speed are varied by the first swimmer.

Diving with a Partner
Two partners dive together and signal the "O" signal (OK) to each other. Then they swim a distance underwater before they resurface.
Variations:
- First of all the partners swim on the surface. After covering a distance of about 8m they signal the "O" sign to each other and then dive underwater and swim a distance before they resurface using the same sign as above.
- The partners swim along and dive underwater at regular intervals.
- Three or four partners swim along and dive down after arranging beforehand when to do so.

Pushing Competition
Two partners hold onto a swimming board so that it is between the two of them. They are on the centerline of the pool. Using the crawl leg kick they now try to push the other to one's own side of the pool.

Variations:
- Doing it wearing one flipper.
- Doing it using the butterfly leg kick and a single flipper.
- Doing it with two people at each end of the swimming board.
- Underwater pushing competition with snorkel equipment.

Group Pushing Competition

Two groups are standing with members partnered off on the centerline of the pool opposite each other. They hold swimming boards between them. When each person takes hold of the board to his left with his left hand and holds the one to the right with his right hand, then this takes the form of a zipper. Each group now tries to push the other to his side of the pool.

Variations:
- Doing it wearing one flipper.
- Pushing by using the leg action of the butterfly stroke.

Running and Catching Games – originally played as such but here played wearing flippers:

"What's the time Mr. Shark?", "Chain Catch", "Fisherman, Fisherman - How deep is the water?", "Ox on the Hill 1,2,3" and other running and catching games (see RHEKER 2004 "Aquafun - Games and Fun for the Advanced" pp 69-73).

Diving Games with a Diving Mask

First of all some simple games are carried out in the beginners' pool so that the children are able to use the mask on the surface and underwater safely. Later, games and game forms are carried out in deeper water.

Diving with a Mask in the Beginners' Pool

The swimmers put the mask on and find out how to orient themselves in the beginners' pool.

Variations:
- One of the partners, who isn't wearing a mask, accompanies the diver on his reconnaissance tour.
- Two swimmers, both wearing a mask, find their way round the beginners' pool together.

The divers meet up in the beginners' pool and give each other underwater signs.

The divers dive down in the beginners' pool and collect 'treasures' from the bottom (diving rings, underwater polo balls, diving stones etc.).

Diving with a Mask and Flippers in the Main Pool

The swimmers put on a diving mask and flippers and find out how to orient themselves in the main pool.

Variations: See above.

Heading Objects

Different objects (large balls, water polo balls, pull buoys, swimming boards etc.,) are headed up to the surface while the swimmer is wearing a mask and flippers.

Variations:

- The objects are moved in a different manner.
- Heading objects in a relay race.
- Several objects are brought up at once.

Giving Signs Underwater

Each partner dives down and gives the other one an underwater sign.

Variations:

- One partner gives underwater signs and the other one only answers with the "O.K." sign.
- Several underwater signs are exchanged.
- Giving underwater signs in a relay race.
- Silent Post underwater: 6-8 persons wearing snorkeling equipment swim round in a circle. Two of them dive down and one of them gives the other a message consisting of several underwater signs as 'Silent Post'. The receiver passes this message on to another person who dives down and so on until the message gets through all the persons.

Copy-cat in Partners

Two children dive down as partners. One of them does certain movements, which the other has to copy.

Variations:

- One of the partners does a movement underwater, which the other one has to copy as a 'mirror' reflection.

- One of the partners moves around underwater using different techniques. The other partner follows him like a shadow and copies all the movements.

Stone, Paper, Scissors
Two children dive down as partners and they play the game of "Stone, Paper, Scissors". Whoever wins may resurface first.
Variation:
- The game is played three times. The winner gets a plus point.

Underwater Arithmetic
Two children dive down as partners. Underwater, one partner gives the other an arithmetical problem using his fingers.

Clearing the Mask
The diving mask is taken off underwater and the water that has got inside is cleared and then put on again. To learn this technique, first of all put the head underwater wearing the diving mask, then flood it with water. Afterwards, take the head in the hand by the back of the neck, press the upper rim of the mask against the forehead and breathe out through the nose into the inside of it. Doing this pushes the water out of the mask so that it is filled with air again.
Variations:
- The mask is taken off underwater in the main pool and the water that has filled it is blown out as you put it on again.
- The mask is thrown into the water. The diver has to dive down now and put the mask on clearing it as he does.
- The mask and snorkel are thrown into the water. The diver now has to dive down, put the mask on underwater, clear it and blow the snorkel free after resurfacing.

Swapping Masks
Two divers dive down together. Underwater they take the diving mask off and swap it with each other. They first of all carry out the exchange when the mask has been cleared of water.
Variations:
- The mask and the snorkel are exchanged.
- All the pieces of the snorkel equipment are exchanged.

Tying Knots

A ribbon or little rope is knotted to a diving ring while diving underwater (c.f., HOFFMAN, 1995, pp 4-41).

Variations:

Various types of knots are used.

One of the partners dives down and knots a ribbon. The other one has to untie the knot.

Diving Games with the Snorkel

In these games the following skills are learned and practiced:

- Breathing through the snorkel.
- Breathing through the snorkel while swimming on the surface.
- After diving down and resurfacing, blowing the snorkel clear.

Breathing through the Snorkel

In the beginners' pool, the divers put the snorkel in their mouths and breathe through it.

Variations:

- Standing in the beginners' pool the divers put the snorkel in their mouths and breathe through it.
- With their heads underwater in the beginners' pool, the divers put the snorkel in their mouth and breathe through it.
- Swimming with the snorkel and the head in water.
- After resurfacing the snorkel is blown clear.

Target Shooting with the Snorkel

Swimming boards are stood up, resting angled against each other, at the edge of the pool. From a distance from the edge, selected by the player, he attempts to knock the boards down by using water sprayed out of the snorkel. Who can knock down the most boards?

Variations:

- Increase the distance from the edge.
- Doing it as a relay race.
- Doing it as a team competition: Which team can knock 10 swimming boards down first?
- The targets can be altered:
- Hit pull buoys.
- Spray into a bucket.

The Chieftain
Swim with the mask on back to front and at the same time breathe through the snorkel. This is so you learn to breathe through the mouth without getting water up your nose (c.f., LÜCHTENBERG, 1995, p 98).

Swapping Snorkels
Two children swim along on the surface using one snorkel. As soon as one of them doesn't have any more air, the other has to pass his snorkel across to him. The snorkel is exchanged often and it has to be done so that the head remains underwater.
Variations:
• One of the partners dives and the other snorkels along.
• The snorkel is exchanged at set intervals.
• The distances are increased.
• Three people snorkel along as partners with one snorkel between them.

Breathing Holes
Several hoops (gymnastic hoops, car tire inner tubes etc.,) are laid around on the water. Now, everyone dives wearing masks and snorkels. They may only resurface up through the hoops, which represent 'breathing holes'. The breathing holes must be vacated quickly.
Variations:
• Use fewer hoops.
• Use fewer hoops than participants.
• Only one diver may surface in any one hoop.
• Instead of hoops, swimming boards, floating on the surface, can be used as a 'breathing bar'.

Diving Games with the Full Snorkel Equipment
In this section, swimming and diving with the full set of snorkeling equipment is supposed to be learned with the help of games.

Swimming with Full Snorkel Equipment
Everyone swims with the full snorkel equipment on the surface of the water.
Variations:
• Swimming with the full snorkel equipment with the back crawl.

- Swimming with the full snorkel equipment in a sidestroke position.
- Increasing the distance to be swum.
- Swimming with the full snorkel equipment in a relay race.
- Diving underwater with the full snorkel equipment on the tummy, back and sidestroke position.
- Changing over the snorkel on the surface to diving underwater.

Using the Snorkel in Waves
All swim, each with a partner, with the full snorkel equipment on the surface. At an agreed signal they dive underwater and swim a distance and then give a joint sign to resurface, blow their snorkels clear and continue using the snorkel on the surface. After this they dive down underwater again.

Sandwich Snorkel
Two people as partners snorkel and dive alternately. The one partner dives first of all, while the other one snorkels on the surface. As soon as the first one surfaces, the second one begins to dive underwater.
Variations:
- Both the people have only one snorkel between them so that when the changeover occurs they have to pass the snorkel over.
- The diving partner swims on his back directly underneath the snorkeler.

Leading the Blind
One of the partners dives with a blacked-out mask and is lead by the seeing partner round the pool.
Variations:
- Dive around obstacles.
- Underwater course in which you swim around by feeling. As you are going along you have to guess what the objects are by feeling them.
- Collecting underwater 'treasures'.

Follow your Partner
One of the partners dives and swims underwater with a lead of 5m. The second partner dives along after him and tries to catch him.
Variations:
- The first diver thinks up different diving and swimming techniques he can do: the crawl leg kick on the tummy and on the back,

butterfly leg kick, other leg kicks and arm movements etc.). The person following has to copy these techniques.
- Move along in different ways, change direction, alter the depth at which they are diving etc.

Mirror Images in Diving

Two children dive down as partners, swimming underwater alongside each other. The second partner does all the movements and changes into the direction which the other one chooses.

Variations:
- The first diver thinks up different diving and swimming techniques he can do.
- Diving and swimming in different position styles.
- Move along in different ways, change direction, alter the depth at which they are diving etc.
- Changing the swimming speed.

Diving under Icebergs

Several obstacles are placed in the water representing *icebergs* (swimming boards, pull buoys, air beds etc.). Everyone has to dive under these *icebergs*, making sure that when they resurface they don't come up under an *iceberg*.

Variations:
- The *icebergs* can be moved out of the way using the head.
- The *icebergs* can be lifted up and thrown high out of the water with the head.

Timed Diving

One of the partners dives underwater while the other counts the time. Who can stay underwater five, six or 10 seconds?

(**Note:** Individual monitoring is mandatory. Sufferers of hyperventilation may not take part).

Variations:
- Who can dive the longest?
- Who can breathe out the longest when diving?
- Two partners dive underwater while a third watches on the surface.

Distance Diving

Who can dive underwater with snorkel equipment the farthest?
Caution: When doing distance diving, there must be **supervision** for every diver present. Sufferers of hyperventilation may not take part.
Variations:

- Diving underwater for a length.
- Who can dive underwater for more than a length?
- Diving without snorkel equipment.
- Diving underwater after diving in headfirst.
- Distance diving with flippers.
- When diving underwater down the distance, you have to collect objects from the water.
- Diving underwater round underwater slalom poles.

Swimming like a Screw

Everyone is swimming on the surface with snorkel equipment and they turn with a longitudinal screw turn of the body. Who can do four screw turns from the tummy to the back position in a length and return?
Variations:

- Lengthen the distance for swimming the 'screw'.
- Who can do the most screw turns?
- Screw turn swimming as a relay.
- Screw turn swimming as a diver underwater.

Pulling Water Buckets

Who can pull a water bucket diving underwater with snorkel equipment?
Variations:

- Lengthen the distance the bucket has to be pulled.
- Pulling a bucket as a relay.

Underwater Somersault

Everyone is swimming with snorkel equipment on the surface of the water. They then dive down and try to do a somersault underwater.
Variations:

- Who can do the most somersaults?
- Who can do a somersault with a screw turn?
- Who can do a forwards somersault followed by a backwards somersault?

- Who can do the most somersaults with screw turns longitudinally?
- Who can do an underwater loop?
- Looping backwards: From lying on your back, stretch over into a backward arc and back under to a position lying on the back.
- Looping forwards: From lying on your tummy, stretch over into a forward arc and back into a position lying on the tummy.

Guessing Figures

Various objects are laid down on the bottom underwater so that they form figures. The children have to dive underwater from figure to figure and try to recognize which figure is represented.

Putting on the Snorkel Equipment

Flippers, mask and snorkel are laid down underwater on the bottom. The diver has to dive down and put them on underwater.
Variations:

- Only put the flippers on.
- Only put the mask on, clear it and resurface.
- Put the mask on, clear it, resurface and blow the snorkel clear.
- Put on all the snorkel equipment.
- Put on all the snorkel equipment and clear the mask.
- Put on all the snorkel equipment, clear the mask and blow the snorkel clear.

Swapping Flippers

Two divers, who have the same flipper size and wearing snorkel equipment, dive underwater and swap over the flippers.
Variations:

- Swap the flippers over at different depths.
- Swapping flippers in groups of three.
- Swapping flippers done as a relay.

Swapping Snorkel Equipment

Two divers, wearing snorkel equipment, dive underwater and swap over the flippers, the mask and the snorkel.
Variations:

- Only swap over the masks underwater.
- Only swap over the flippers and the snorkel.

- Swap over all the snorkel equipment.
- Swap over all the snorkel equipment at different depths.
- Swapping over all the snorkel equipment in groups of three.
- Swapping over all the snorkel equipment as a relay.

2.1.9 'Little Games' as Underwater Ball Games

At this point, games and game forms are introduced to practice and familiarize the pupils with the underwater polo ball and go on to games of underwater polo, which can take place as a competition.

First of all, carrying the underwater polo ball is addressed and practiced using carrying games, before we go on to practice passing and catching the underwater polo ball as a team. Playing with opponents is introduced in the 'Tiger Ball Games'.

The target games of 'underwater polo' and 'underwater rugby' are introduced in a simple form so that they can be played by several groups without a lot of trouble.

Carrying the Underwater Polo Ball
Who can dive underwater with the underwater polo ball for the furthest distance?
Variations:
- Carrying the ball underwater for a width of the main pool.
- Carrying the ball underwater for a length of the main pool as far as you can.
- Carrying the ball underwater wearing flippers.
- Carrying the ball underwater wearing the full snorkel equipment.
- Carrying the ball underwater as a relay.
- Carrying the ball underwater around obstacles.

Underwater Polo Marathon
3-5 members of a team try to carry the underwater polo ball as far as possible. The first diver dives down and carries the ball as far as possible and then drops it down. The next one takes it from there. Which group can cover the longest distance?

Variations:
- If each player can dive twice, which group can dive the longest distance?
- Which group can do the exercise diving round obstacles?

Underwater Polo Ultra-Marathon

3-5 members of a team try to carry the underwater polo ball as far as possible. The first diver dives down and carries the ball as far as he can and then passes it to a partner, who has been following him using a snorkel on the surface. The snorkeler now dives underwater and passes it on to the next one etc. The underwater polo ball must always be under the water. No one may surface with the ball. Which group can cover the longest distance?

Treasure Hunting Underwater

Different objects (diving rings, diving stones, 'treasures', and underwater polo balls) are distributed around the main swimming pool. The players are divided into two teams lined up on opposite sides of the pool, and on a signal each one tries to collect as many objects as one can for the own team by putting them into a basket underwater.

Variations:
- Each player may collect only one object each time.
- Treasure hunting done as a relay: One player in each team starts to seek out the treasures. As soon as he lays the object by his team the second one starts.
- Pirate Game: As long as the object is being carried in the water, they can chase and catch the others.

Passing the Underwater Polo Ball

All the players, wearing snorkel equipment underwater, form a circle and pass an underwater polo ball amongst themselves. After passing the ball each one can surface to take a breath.

Variations:
- Two underwater polo balls are used.
- The ball is passed to the player two away in the circle.
- Ball Chase: Two balls are being played in the circle. The players with even numbers play against the uneven numbered players.

Simple Underwater Polo Ball Passing Game

3-5 players pass the ball underwater to each other. The person holding the ball may not surface. The passes must therefore be done underwater. The team that wins is the one that achieves the most passes.

Variations:

- Time playing: Which team can pass the ball correctly underwater for the longest time?
- The opposing team can use a defender to disturb the passing done by the other team.

Underwater "Tiger Ball"

5-8 players form a circle and pass the ball to each other underwater. The players being passed to may not surface. The passes must therefore be done underwater. An opponent ("tiger") stands in the middle of the circle and tries to catch the ball or deflect it. If he manages to do this then the person who passed the ball goes into the middle as the new "tiger".

Variations:

- The number of 'tigers' is increased: First of all you start with two tigers and then 3 or 4.
- The game is played in two circles - team against team. The 'tiger' comes from the opposing team each time - with changeovers from the home team each time a ball is caught. The winning team is the one that has had the most tigers in the opposing team's circle.
- The number of 'tigers' is increased until there are as many tigers as there are players in the circle (see the Normal Underwater Polo Ball Passing Game).

Normal Underwater Polo Ball Passing Game

Two teams of 3-6 players each play against each other. They try to keep the ball in their own ranks by passing it to each other underwater. The person passing may not surface to do the pass. The passes must therefore be done underwater. The winner is the team to achieve 10 passes underwater.

Variations:

- Which team can achieve 20 passes first?
- Time playing: Which team can keep possession of the ball for the longest time?

- A few underwater polo rules are introduced (see below).
- After 10 passes, an additional point can be scored, by placing it in a basket underwater.

'Big Games' as Underwater Ball Games   2.1.10

After the game using the underwater polo ball has been learned using the little games, underwater polo and underwater rugby can be introduced. The game is first of all done along simplified rules.

Underwater polo

Underwater polo is played in a swimming pool with a depth of between 3.5 - 5m. The playing area size is between 12 x 8m and 18 x 12m.

Two teams, each of 5 players and a goalkeeper, play in this three-dimensional area. The teams are distinguished by wearing different bathing suits (dark or white) and different colored bathing caps. Each team tries to get an underwater polo ball filled with saltwater into the opposing team's basket.

All the players are wearing snorkel equipment (flippers, diving masks and snorkels). Only the person in ball possession may be attacked in order to wrest the ball off him. Unfair play (kicking, strangling, ripping off the other's snorkel/bathing equipment etc.,) is forbidden and is punished by giving a penalty shot or a time out penalty.

Variations:
- Play in shallow water - depth 2m (for beginners).
- No hindrance or attacking the opposing player is permitted.
- The game is played with smaller teams (3:3).
- The game rules are increased so that foul rules are introduced etc.

Underwater Rugby

Underwater rugby is an official competitive game, played with the following rules:

Playing area: Swimming pool with a depth of 3.5 - 5m.
Size of playing area: The playing area size is between 12 x 8m and 18 x 12m.

Teams: Each team consists of 5 players and a goalkeeper. There are also 5 reserves. The teams are distinguished by wearing different colored special bathing caps fitted with ear protectors. They also wear different colored swimming costumes and possibly neoprene armbands.

The Game: Each team tries to get an underwater ball filled with saltwater into the opposing team's basket. All the players are wearing snorkel equipment (flippers, diving masks and snorkels). Only the person in ball possession may be attacked in order to wrest the ball off him. Unfair play (kicking, strangling, ripping off the other's snorkel/bathing equipment etc.,) is forbidden and is punished by giving a penalty shot or a time out penalty. If the person in possession of the ball runs out of air, he has to pass the ball or let it drop and then surface to get air.

Referees: Two referees with air bottles control the game underwater. There is also one referee out of the water.

Underwater Hockey

Underwater Hockey is not an official competitive game. However, it is an interesting game that can be adapted from the way it's played on the pitch outside or in the hall, so that it can be played in a swimming pool underwater environment.

Underwater hockey can be played along the following simplified rules:
Two teams of four to six players, using a short wooden bat try to get a diving ring into the opponent's goal.
Variations:
- Play the game in shallower water (for beginners).
- Play it in deeper water 2-5m deep.
- Play where opponents are not allowed to be tackled.
- Play with different size teams: 3:3, 5:5, 6:6.
- The game rules are extended to include the foul rule etc.
- Play with hockey sticks and an underwater puck (lead disc).

Getting a Taste for Underwater Diving with Equipment (F. DUNSCHEN)

2.2

"Water moves, but not without a reason"

African proverb

Introduction

2.2.1

Diving using compressed air is a very special experience. At this point, we cannot go into detail with diving with compressed air. Nevertheless, there has enough basic information been summarized here to allow to try diving with equipment. With this there will be a unique impulse to make it possible to come to terms with one's own body and the environment. A general instructor can prepare one for diving with equipment (see Snorkel diving, Apnoe diving (free-diving without air bottles)). When actually carrying it out, it must be done in conjunction with a trained diving instructor. The high challenging character of this type of sport makes it an ideal choice as a project. Its relativity to other various subjects is quite obvious, so that interdisciplinary instruction can be considered.

The sport of underwater diving can be categorized as belonging to the group of adventure sports. Within this group, there are a number of extreme sports (e.g., parachuting, rafting, climbing amongst others). Diving is often categorized by the non-divers as an extreme sport, but compared with today's leisure sport diving, this is not exactly correct. Leisure diving means diving with snorkels (basic equipment: Flippers, Diving mask and Snorkel), Apnoe diving and diving using compressed air. However, every type of diving has its own different prerequisites for the abilities and skills needed. Generally, as a rule, before one dives with compressed air, sufficient knowledge and skills should be gained doing snorkeling and Apnoe diving. Diving as a sport began after the construction of the first artificial lung (respiratory controlled delivery system or second phase of the breathing apparatus) in 1943 by COUSTEAU, which was the turning point for free diving. Nowadays, diving has developed to be a very popular sport and looks like gaining even more popularity as continuing improvement of equipment and instruction makes diving more and more safe.

2.2.2 Theoretical Aspects

When looking at the characteristics of the sport of swimming, the adventure and experience gained in diving can add a few positive aspects to the features.

The experience of observing nature with its flora and fauna associated with diving has not been accounted for in the following paragraphs. This is because beginners' training for diving is limited to taking place in the halls of the swimming baths. Moving forwards on one's own and staying underwater provides the beginner diver with sufficient impressions of adventure. The motor senses are already challenged enough for the pupils, that an additional distraction by an exotic environment can be regarded as a disadvantage or that alternatively, on the other hand, instruction in the swimming baths has clear advantages.

Amongst other things, the training is aimed at imparting instruction in specific diving knowledge as a prerequisite for taking note of the necessary ways of conducting oneself in diving (see also The Basics of Underwater Diving with Equipment - Chapter 2.1.6. and 2.1.7.).

Adequate knowledge permits being able to stay underwater with the least of dangers and, in part, also gives unique experience of the body and individual by that status i.e., diving:

➢ Individual *experience of success* through confrontation and achievement of tasks considered to be demanding:
  • New interests.
  • Of an adventurous character, learning to take risks and controlling the risk-taking.
  • Improvement of individual capacity to act.
➢ Sport with a Partner
  • Feeling responsible/sharing responsibility with the diving partner.
  • Group experience/Team spirit, without any performance ambitions in the foreground.
➢ Very *high challenge characteristic* through association with the value of experience of that particular sport
  • Having fun in the sense of experiencing a flow of adventure

through the achievement of tasks considered to be demanding and the time spent with movement underwater.
➤ Incentive for new discoveries or improvement of *the body system*
  • Floating in a three-dimensional space (weightlessness with good counter-balance) initiates new processes of perception. Understanding the different physical functions of the body and ways of reacting.
➤ Relaxation while being underwater and at the end of a physical exertion
  • Relaxation with correct breathing made more conscious by being underwater.

The special features of the sport of diving have been proved to be helpful for the therapy of psychologically ill people (DUNSCHEN 1998, p 40). The particular fields of experience and the possible lessons learned connected with the basic training of diving have a positive influence on some symptoms of physical illnesses.

Fresh experiences are possible in diving, like also the medical dangers, because of its close connection with the physical properties of water.

At comparative temperatures, water has approximately a density of about 800 times of that of air. This means that the pressure in a 10 m high pillar of water is the same on the diver as the earth's atmosphere. The higher density of water gives other physical properties. Water provides 3,400 times more heat capacity and 25 times greater heat conductivity than air.

The human organism is subject to different physical laws during the diving process. It is very necessary to take note of these natural laws. Each dive carried out can be divided into a *compression phase (increasing pressure)*, a phase of *equal (constant)* pressure and a *decompression phase (decreasing pressure)*. In the compression phase there is the danger of low pressure trauma. The equal pressure phase conceals the danger of a toxic breathing effect. Above all, in the decompression phase there is an overpressure trauma and an increase in the soluble gases in the blood. These phases are important.

With Apnoe diving, in the surfacing phase or when swimming distances, above all, in cases preceded by hyperventilation there is a danger of hypoxia.

According to the Archimedes principle, the loss of weight of a body when immersed in water is equal to the weight of fluid it displaces (DE MAREES 1992, p 255). By virtue of an adequate counter-balance, the human being is in a position to create a so-called hydrostatic balance that results in a state of suspense of the body in water.

This state of suspense permits unlimited three-dimensional movements to be made, where these can be done at individually desired speeds and in all axial directions of the body. In comparison to the resistance of air, water resistance provides a more tactile and more kinesthetic perception as a sensory response to the movements performed. Intensive bodily experiences in a three-dimensional space are possible by virtue of a greater than above-average motivation to do them.

Without the technical possibility of being able to carry a supply of air and its regulated delivery, breathing underwater would lead to an intake of water into the lungs with its equivalent serious results. One is very conscious of the fact that the automatic process of breathing in a normal environment is replaced for humans by an unnatural process underwater. Acoustic, visual and vestibular processes of perception underwater all give immediate feedback concerning breathing and its influence on numerous other processes.

Breathing in when diving is very audible and, as per the Archimedes principle, this leads to an upwards movement or a slowing down of a sinking movement of the whole body. Breathing out can also be heard as an audible sound and leads to a movement of the body in the opposite direction. The air breathed out is clearly visible and audible as it rises to the surface of the water.

Because of the higher density of water, visibility and hearing are generally altered in comparison with these faculties on dry land.

The impulse trigger in the hearing center of the brain is strained because the speed of sound underwater is 4 times the normal, and this impedes the direction of sound (DE MAREES 1992, p257). The drop in sound out of the air is very little and the sources of sound underwater are generally reduced, other than the pressure assisted expelling of air and the ascending bubbles breathed out. A qualitatively sufficient acoustic noise for the ears, as a prerequisite for verbal communication, will only be successful if the skulls of the divers touch each other directly and the sound waves transferred in this manner. This kind of communication is however only useful for experiments and is rather unimportant for proper use. A greater distance makes communication through the mouthpiece of the air bottle almost impossible and guessing or association of what might have been said is only possible in some situations if one has made enough experiences with it.

The best known and most often used form of communication underwater is the *sign language*, while signs made up or agreed between partners are also used.

Visible perception is, however, also affected, because objects seen through the diving mask appear nearer and magnified by 1/3rd . Many divers do not consciously remember this fact.

In addition, there is the tactile feeling needed for moving about a space; blind divers show underwater for example that they are impressively capable in their freedom of movement and orientation capabilities, while, on dry land, most of them are fearful of bumping into things and have fear of hurting themselves. GERSTENBRAND (1997, p 93) emphasizes the importance of a sound functioning central nervous system, "equally for the control of the changes and drop in the motor system, caused by the partial weightlessness and a heightened state of water pressure. There is also the need to process information concerning the environment that the body is in, using merely the partial functioning of the human perception organs still in their land adaptation mode".

The aim of diving instruction for the sport as a leisure item is to school a form of economic movements underwater. The diving time should not be shortened by doing rapid movements which increase the air expenditure, but the individual should have the time to consciously realize the changed environmental situation one is in. Physiologically, the beginner diver's organism is mainly placed on demand at a medium level, which is governed by the intensity and extent (also by the frequency) of the exercises contained in the individual practice sessions.

In diving, it is the characteristic of a high challenge that comes out of the described possibilities of experiencing adventure together with its attractiveness and excitement, rather than the aspects of rivalry and competition that appear in numerous other sporting fields of an equally challenging nature.

In leisure diving it is not the performance that is the center point of interest, but more the aspect of experience. This creates a good framework for learning about cooperation and partnership. Diving is a "buddy" sport where responsibility for the safety principles of every diving practice is shared with that partner.

Considering the characteristics described for this kind of sport, it will, however be clear that the diver has to rely on a technique that is, first of all, used in a strange new 'world'. The feeling of having to rely on something and the strain caused by so many new impressions and perceptions of emotion can lead to a feeling of anxiousness. This situation has to be met in diving by using a step-by-step introduction (the mastering of the snorkel is a must) and strictly sticking to the safety rules, as well as only ever diving with a partner. In this way, diving with air bottles can be a very positive experience giving lifelong memories or you could even turn out to become a diving instructor oneself and make diving a hobby.

2.2.3　The First Exercises in Diving using Compressed Air

Note: Confidence in the use of the basic equipment (snorkel) is an absolute prerequisite for diving with equipment. The ability to be able to dive safely is a consequence of learning movements and coming to terms with the theoretical aspects of diving, which can be practiced in exercises and made clear by experimentation. When choosing exercises, one should take care that beginners don't feel overtaxed and have the opportunity to express their points and reflect on their actions. Complex game forms are only useful and sensible when the ability to stay underwater and move about with air bottles has been comprehensively automated. In the following section, therefore, the first impressions of automated diving will correspondingly be at the forefront.

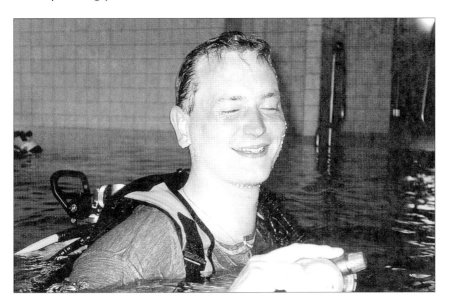

Picture 6: *Satisfaction after a dive*

Breathing underwater

Before doing this exercise, everyone should have tried out on dry land, how it feels to breathe through the second stage of the air regulator. The diving instructor positions himself on the bottom of the pool in a non-swimmer area with a second air bottle. One after the other of the participants dive for the air bottle and breathe with it underwater. After an agreed sign to surface, they resurface breathing out and change over. The monitoring diving instructor can com-municate with the divers using the underwater sign language.

Variations:

- In a second run through, the participants try to lay down on the bottom of the pool by exhaling deeply (- because of the different buoyancy factors of the pupils' bodies, this is a difficult exercise - an aid to this can be a weight lying on the floor that they can hold on to).

- By breathing in, they try to suspend themselves or balance above the bottom of the pool without any other movements.
- Arithmetic questions to be answered are set underwater so that the pupils' attention is distracted onto other things.

Picture 7: *Instructions prior to diving with an air bottle.*

Getting into the water with an air bottle

The air bottle, dependent on its volume, weighs at least 10 kg, to which one must add the other pieces of equipment and this makes moving about on dry land not an awful lot of pleasure. It also requires a particular way necessary for getting into the water.

- Get into the water from the edge lying down flat or pulling yourself in.

Variations:

- Jump into the water feet first. As you do, push your heels downwards or in other words pull the tips of the flippers up towards the knees. Hold onto the diving mask by keeping it pressed to the forehead with one hand.
- From a sitting position on the edge of the pool, let yourself fall backwards into the water thinking about holding the diving mask as you do so.

Moving forwards underwater with the air bottle
After an explanation on how to put the equipment on, the participants move around accompanying each other at various depths through the water. They move about in three-dimensions as well as do movements about the axis of their bodies and other movement combinations without time pressure.

Breathing underwater without the diving mask
Breathing through the mouth under the water, and with the nose underwater, requires some practice (c.f., the reflexes).

Clearing the diving mask
Clearing the mask was already learned during the exercises with the snorkel. The participants can experience that it is a lot easier to clear the diving mask using an air bottle instead of diving with a snorkel because of the practically unlimited air one can have. It should be noted that to do this, the head has to be pulled backwards into the neck.

Exercises to get a picture of the changing pressure
In snorkeling, it was already possible to learn how to recognize the effects of pressure. This can be done by diving with flexible objects (i.e., balloons) and sometimes rigid ones filled with air (e.g., tins which can be closed tight using cling-foil or 'Tupperware" containers).

When diving with an air bottle, this can be easily observed at one's ease. Following on from this, group discussions regarding what has been observed can be gone through and a relationship made with those hollow spaces filled with air in the human body (middle ear, lungs etc.).
Variations:
- The observations can be recorded underwater using a pencil (you can write with this underwater), to include also sketches of the processes.
- A dive is made well down into the depths (about 3 m) so that the pressure bursts the cling-foil over the opening of the tin.
- A balloon is filled with air underwater and it is watched as it surfaces.

Recovering objects using air

A diving ring or similar heavy object is tied to a bucket, which is filled with water and sunk into the water. The divers breathe out air so that, as it rises, it collects into the bucket, eventually also lifting up the bucket.

Variation:

Dependent on the weight of the object used, the participants feed only sufficient air into the bucket until it is suspended, motionless, in the water.

Diving through an underwater course

An underwater course is set up using weights, gymnastic hoops, slalom poles etc., and this has to be dived through, while a partner watches.

Variation:

Using underwater sign language, the companion tells the diver which way to go through the course.

The Impulses for Creative and Playful Jumping and Diving into the Water

2.3

"Do not rebuke the river if you fall into the water."

(Korean saying)

Introduction

2.3.1

Jumping, diving and dipping into the water are things we can only experience with the element of water. The changeover between the very different elements of air and water give lasting experiences. While we hardly notice the air which surrounds us, being in water brings the feeling of being enveloped on all sides with it, because we are intensively conscious of it. We arrive at a direct dialog between our own bodies and the world surrounding us and this leads to physical and psychological sensations and the urge to move and learn.

Diving into water makes this changeover in the elements particularly clear. Gliding along in water is a pleasant feeling, but splatting down onto water after a flopped dive is sometimes accompanied with pain.

Jumping and diving into the water offers lots of opportunities to form creative movements. This is why jumping in and diving are very popular with children. Children can make fundamental, movement experiences as they jump or dive into water: Jumping in using one or both legs, flying through the air when diving, floating in the water and in the air, dipping various parts of their body in water etc.

At the same time, jumping and diving into water schools or improves one's ability to coordinate as well as the ability to orient oneself and maintain one's balance.

This area of swimming instruction - jumping and diving into water - fulfills different pedagogic aims and therefore has to be covered with different aspects in mind.

Jumping and diving into water has the following pedagogic aspects:

The ability to be aware, develop experience in movements
When jumping in and diving, the perception of one's own body can be experienced afresh and improved. Unique bodily experiences can be made: One can carry out movements in the air without contact with the ground. All senses of the body can be experienced: Dipping all parts of the body into water, splatting down onto the water, making a clean entry into the water when diving, hearing and seeing, tasting different qualities of water.

The ways of moving can be increased by learning new movement sequences such as jumping in from a springboard, doing a flying jump or dive, diving in, diving headfirst and doing a somersault as you dive in etc.

The ability to express oneself with the body and create movements
Jumping and diving into water allow you to create movements that are very creative, impressive and bold.

To be adventurous and yet responsible
Right from the first jump into the water from the pool steps up to diving in from the high board, will-power and courage is demanded. For every new type of jump or dive from a new different height, but especially diving off rocks, an adventurous situation is to the fore.

To experience being able to perform something, understand it and judge it correctly
After having done a successful or even a flopped jump or dive, you are immediately able to assess your performance and judge it. Seen from the aspect of performance and ability, jumping and diving into water also promotes self-confidence and courage in children.

To be able to cooperate, be competitive and be able to communicate
When jumping in and diving with a partner, helping others when learning new jumps of dives and other group tasks, cooperation and understanding are necessary. Being competitive is something, which can be seen in the comparative results of artistic and high diving.

To promote health and develop health consciousness.
In order to be able to develop a health consciousness, one has to be aware of the dangers and risks and judge these correctly.

So that jumping in and diving is successful from the aspect of the various educational aims, at the beginning of the chapter several examples of the approach to freely constructed jumps and dives will be given.

However, there are several safety precautions that have to be noted. Equally important, a well-thought out procedure must be employed to ensure that no pupil is overstrained and that each can have a learning experience according to their individual level of ability. This is necessary so that a suitable starting level can be found.

Jumping in and diving, which can be classified primarily as the interpretation of *aesthetics, style, expression, courage, performance and ability,* can be organized to include games and game forms.

Basics regarding Jumping in and Diving

Already in the first swimming lessons on jumping in and diving, the children have to learn some mandatory safety rules:
- Only jump in or dive when the surface of the water is free
- Only jump in or dive in when the instructor gives a sign
- No running jumps or dives may be done because of the high risk of slipping
- Curl the toes round the edge of the pool to avoid slipping

No diving headfirst into the learner's pool – this is very dangerous!

The ability *to jump in and dive* while swimming for beginners is aimed, above all, to facilitate the following general aims:

1. Having fun while jumping in and diving
2. Increasing the feeling of safety in the water
3. Reducing fear and inhibitions, and promoting self-confidence
4. Developing the decision-making ability and will-power
5. Gaining various experiences with the movements
6. Promoting control of the body
7. Learning about space
8. Learning to follow instructions

The basics for jumping and diving into water were already set in beginners' swimming. There are many games and exercises that can give a lot of fun for non-swimmers in the beginners' pool (c.f., Volume 1 "Aquafun - First Steps" RHEKER 2004, pp 157-168).

Building on these elementary experiences of hopping and jumping and diving, the joy in doing it can be broadened and the various movement experiences as a beginner can be extended. Preparations for artistic and high board diving can be made using these popular skills. The games and playful exercises for jumping and diving take on a special value.

The start of jumping and diving and the basis for sports diving are rooted in the elementary experiences gained in beginners' swimming:

➤ First of all, the children learn by hopping and jumping up and down in the water and taking one foot off the pool floor for a short while.

➤ In the next step they learn to dive by starting jumping and diving in at the different levels of the pool steps. These exercises for diving can also be done from a ladder placed in the beginners' pool. These jumps prepare one for jumping and diving in from the edge of the pool.

➤ Jumping in from the edge of the beginners' pool is great fun and can be combined with various exercises and game forms to have even more joy. Subsequently, these movement exercises that promote creative jumping have their own value.

➤ Similarly, jumping in with a partner or as a group increases the preparedness, the courage and the fun in jumping in.

➤ Preparation for jumping and diving from the 1-m board can be done by starting with simple jumps from the edge of the main pool.

➤ Using popular jumps and dives, which can be found in many games and exercises, partner and group jumps and dives can be introduced.

➤ From the area of artistic diving from the springboard or high board, the methodical introduction to the head first jump and the somersault, as the first artistic dives done, is shown by giving examples.

➤ Funny and adventurous jumps conclude this chapter.

Diving as a Learning Process towards an Adventurous Way of Movement

A rejection of learning movements in a technically oriented way in preference to using a varied method of learning to move, which gives an individual schooling of the senses and perceptions, was already covered in Chapter 1.4. Swimming instruction, and the specific area of jumping in and diving, should be made to be a question of learning by experience and learning subjectively how to move in water (c.f., HILDEBRANDT 1999, p 249).

Children are all very different. They can be daring or still very anxious, skilled or awkward. For the subject of jumping in and diving, they approach the instruction, all with different previous experiences. Therefore, for sports and swimming instruction, the prerequisites of the target group have to be taken into consideration. Freely constructed instruction integrates the different experiences and allows an open approach to the environment of water and to the subject of "dipping into this strange element" - namely jumping in and diving. One can speak of a dialog by the individual physique between the medium of water and its specific characteristics. In order for this dialog to be successful and for it to lead on to positive experiences, jumping and diving into the environment of water must take place in a relaxed learning atmosphere.

Fear and joy are the two most important emotions felt when jumping in and diving. Fear leads to strong inhibitions when learning to move. These are often connected to failures or successes. Any anxiety that a child shows should be treated with respect and taken seriously. Pressurizing or demanding more will-power is counter-productive and increases the fear. If the persons are taken seriously with their anxieties and learning experiences, then by using freely constructed movement exercises, successful experiences can be taught in an atmosphere free from stress and these can serve to strengthen self-confidence and effect positive lessons.

A variety of movement possibilities can be learned by using freely constructed exercises. This scenario and freely constructed movement exercises can be carried out at all the various levels of jumping in and diving. They begin with a simple jump into the water and go up to diving in from the edge of the pool and from the 1-m board through to artistic jumps and dives from the springboard or the high board. In this way, the freely constructed jumping and diving movement exercises and scenarios can be combined with all the game forms and games for the different abilities in the following passages.

Here, in brief, are a few movement exercises for jumping in and diving:

Sliding noiselessly into the water
How can I slide my body into the water without making much noise?

First of all, you can try out slipping noiselessly into the water from the steps in the beginners' pool. Different other proven solutions for this are now suggested and the movement exercise broadened to give a new impulse.

Variations:
- Sitting on the edge of the pool let your body slide noiselessly into the water.
- From a standing position on the edge of the pool let your body slide noiselessly down into the water.
- In the main swimming pool, let your body slide down into the water from different heights.
- Let yourself slide down into the pool with a partner.
- From a standing position on the edge of the pool let your body slide noiselessly down into the water and sink down into various different depths.
- From a standing position on the edge of the pool let your body slide noiselessly down into the water and sink down feet or head first into various different depths.
- From a standing position on the edge of the pool let your body slide noiselessly down into the water and glide as far as possible.
- Slide into the pool from a mat or incline on the edge of the pool.

Diving in, leading with different parts of the body into the water
Who can dive into the water leading with different parts of the body?

After the children have tried out with which parts of the body they can lead when diving into the water, the methods can be demonstrated and copied.

Variations:
- Dive in leading with the various parts of the body into the water

while in different starting positions (sitting, standing, lying on the stomach etc).
- Dive in leading with the various parts of the body into the water while carrying out different jumping methods (forwards, backwards etc).
- Dive in with a partner leading with different parts of the body.

Creative jumping displacing lots of water
Who can displace the most water when they jump in (water bomb)?
Who can jump into the water and splash the most people or splash the highest?
Variations:
- Doing the water bomb in different directions: forwards, backwards, sideways.
- Doing the water bomb from different heights and starting positions.
- Doing the water bomb with a partner or a group.

Moving with a partner in the water creatively
Who can do a creative jump in or dive together with a partner?
First of all, various ways to jump in or dive into the water with a partner can be tried out. Then a variety of proven possibilities can be demonstrated and carried out that movement exercises can be broadened by a new impulse.

Picture 8: *A group doing a head dive through hoops*

Creative group movements in the water
How can we as a group do jumps and dives into the water?
Try out various ways and broaden the movement exercise:
Variations:
- The group jumps in or dives in different ways: forwards, backwards, sideways.
- The group jumps in or dives in from different heights and starting positions.
- The group jumps in or dives in all together at the same time.
- The group jumps in or dives in one after the other.
- The group jumps in or dives in with each member doing it differently.

Jumping in or diving in different ways
Who can jump in or dive in different ways?
Variations:
- Doing jumps or dives from different starting positions: From positions of standing, sitting, handstand, or lying on the stomach or back etc.
- Doing jumps or dives in different directions: Forwards, backwards, sideways.
- Doing jumps or dives in different ways from different heights.
- Doing jumps or dives in different ways with a partner or in a group.
- Doing jumps or dives from a suspended position (e.g., with the tips of the feet from the board).

Swinging into the water
A rope is fixed to the ceiling or to the high board. One can now swing over the water and let oneself fall into the water.

Picture 9: *Jumping into the water from a swinging rope*

Funny jumps or dives
Who can do a funny jump or dive?

Various jumps or dives can be tried out to find the funniest one. At the end, some of the more successful ones can be demonstrated as encouragement to the others.

Jumping or diving with equipment
Jumping or diving can be done with different pieces of equipment.
- Jumping in or diving with a small rope.
- Jumping in or diving with a swimming noodle.
- Using an umbrella as a parachute.

Jumping in with a towel
When jumping in let the towel billow up like a parachute.

Jumping in or diving with balls
Who can catch a ball as you jump or dive in? A partner can throw up the ball.
Variations:
- Who can catch a ball, which you throw up yourself?
- Who can catch a ball on the jump and dive in with it?
- Who can catch a ball on the jump and throw it back again while still in the air?
- Who can head the ball away while jumping in?
- The height the ball is thrown can be increased.

Jumping in and Diving in the Beginners' Pool   2.3.3

In preparation for jumping and diving in from the edge of the pool and the 1 m board, first of all the children learn games and game forms about the theme of hopping and jumping into the water in the beginners' pool. When you hop or jump up in the water, the legs leave the bottom of the pool for an initial, short period. This can be done to start with by using a partner to help. The assistance is dropped off, bit by bit, until the children are in a position to be able to jump into the beginners' pool by themselves.

Afterwards, they learn to dive in, by using the various heights of the steps in the pool. Jumping and diving in the beginners' pool has not only the aim of leading up to do this from the springboard or the high board, it also has its own value. Dives with a partner or games in which one is thrown into the water (called in this book - 'thrown jumps') give such a lot of fun and increase one's own motor skills (to be done properly) so that these have a particular value in swimming.

A systematic listing of the simple games and exercises for jumping in the beginners' pool can be found in Volume 1 ("Aquafun - First Steps", RHEKER 2004). Therefore at this point only a few of these will be mentioned. They can be complemented by using partner and thrown jumps.

In order to illustrate the freely constructed exercises possible for the themes above, at the beginning of the chapter, exercises will be explained, which lead up to setting the various movement possibilities. The following games have the theme of hopping and jumping in the beginners' pool.

Freely constructed movement exercises
- Contrast jumping: High - long, loud - quiet, big - small jumps.
- Doing movements and jumps with a partner.
- Jumping into the water, leading with different parts of the body.
- Doing group movements in the water.
- Jumping into the water like animals, athletes or acrobats.

Games in a circle and singing games
"Eenie, Miny, Mo"
All players hold hands and form a circle. One player is the catcher and stands in the middle. Everyone sings and jumps:

"Eenie, Miny, mo,
A fish has bit my toe,
Eeny miny mick
Swim away quick"

After the last word everyone tries to get to or swim to the edge of the pool as quickly as possible, while the catcher tries to catch at least one person before he reaches the edge of the pool. If the catcher is successful, the person caught is the new catcher in the center of the circle.

Variations:

- Everyone sings loudly and jumps up high.
- Everyone singing quietly and making the smallest jump possible.
- All the catchers remain catchers so that the number of catchers increases steadily.

Further singing games in a circle: "Show your feet", "Here we go round the mulberry bush", "Ring-a-ring of roses", "Aram sam sam", "Up I stretch" etc., (see also Volumes 1 & 2).

Acting games

Using movement exercises, the children can be encouraged to be creative and develop their fantasy. By extending the above exercises for movements, the number of games for acting out things can be built on.

Acting like animals

In the exercises, act like the following animals:

- Who can hop through the water like a frog?
- Who can jump like a kangaroo through the water?
- Act like a stork.
- Act like a 'bull in a china shop'.

Acting like athletes

1. In the following exercises, act like athletes in one of their typical "sports postures"
2. Who can hop through the water like a long jumper?
3. Who can hop through the water like a high jumper?
4. Who can act out the gymnast's action?
5. Who can jump through the water like a snow skier?
6. Act out the actions of: a soccer player, basketball player, dancer, trampoline gymnast etc.

Variations:

- Act out the differences between a beginner and a professional sportsman.

- Actions in slow-motion.
- Two athletes jump together synchronized.
- The group acts out the sport.

Guessing what animal
Who can move like an animal through the water?

The others have to guess what animal is being acted. After that, they can all act moving like the animal.

Playing at circuses
The children can act being the different parts of a circus:
Acrobats, clowns, trapeze artistes, jugglers, wild animals.

Further Games:
Relay races: Running relays, hopping relays, obstacle course relays (see RHEKER 2005, pp 74-82)

Jumping with a partner
Jumping and hopping with a partner
One of the partners holds the other by the hands, while he tries out different jumps: Squatting jumps, one-legged jumps, twisting jumps, split-legged jumps etc.
Variations:
- One of the partners tries to do funny jumps.
- Who can splash the most when jumping?
- Who can jump the highest?
- Hopping in different directions: Forwards, backwards, sideways, and diagonally.

Copying jumps
One of the partners thinks up all sorts of jumps and shows them to his partner. The partner has to copy and carry them out in the same way.
Variations:
- The partner does jumps with longitudinal twists (a half-twist, a full twist etc).
- The partner does jumps with longitudinal twists in different directions.

- The partner does jumps with longitudinal twists using different arm movements.
- Jumps with turns in the vertical axis (rolls, and somersaults).
- Jumps with turns at depth.
- Funny jumps.

Jumping at the pool's edge
The children hold on to the edge of the pool and jump up and down.
Variations:
- All try out various jumping styles.
- All hold on with only one hand.
- Everyone jumps up very high.

More Jumps
Free jumping in the beginners' pool.
Everyone jumps around just as they wish.
Variations:
- All hop around on one leg.
- All hop around on both legs.
- Hopping in different directions: Forwards, backwards, sideways, and diagonally.
- Hopping and jumping like animals.

Jumping over obstacles
In the beginners' pool, several obstacles are scattered. The children have to jump over these obstacles.
Variations:
- Poles or ropes are used as obstacles in the water.
- Blocks are built up as obstacles.
- Ropes, tires or poles are held as obstacles at varying heights.

Dolphin jumps and catching dolphins - see Chapter 3.

Thrown up or lift-up jumps
High jump
The jumper puts one foot into the thrower's hand. After a rocking up and down movement of the foot and the hand together, the jumper jumps up very high, propelled by the other's hand.

Variations:
- One of the partners tries funny jumps.
- Who can splash the most when jumping?
- Who jumps the highest?
- Jumping in different directions: Forwards, backwards, sideways, and diagonally.
- Who can jump and make the least splash?
- Who can jump in leading with different parts of the body in the beginners' pool (head first dives are forbidden in the beginners' pool).
- The partner who has dived underwater can actively assist the jump by coming up and helping with it.

Long jump
The jumper places one foot into the hands of the thrower. The jumper now jumps as far as he can with support from his partner.
Variations: see above.

Thrown jump with a special landing
The jumper places one foot into the hands of the thrower. The jumper now jumps with support from his partner in a way so that he has time in the air to prepare a special landing. Headfirst dives are not allowed in the beginners' pool.
Variations: see above.

The screw
The jumper places one foot into the hands of the thrower. The jumper now jumps with support from his partner in a way so that he goes up very high and does one or more longitudinal twists in the air.
Variations: see above.

The thrown jump bomb
The jumper places one foot into the hands of the thrower. The jumper now jumps with support from his partner in a way so that he goes up high and can come down in the water like a bomb.
Variations: see above.

Group thrown jump
Several couples (2-4) grab hold of each other's wrists and form a

launch pad. The jumper places one or both legs on this pad and the throwers launch him upwards into the water.
Variations: see above.

Fish across the table

All the children form a corridor and hold hands with their partner opposite. Now, a child lies down on the hands at the start of the corridor and is moved down over the 'table' to the other end by a lifting up and down of the joined hands. When the end is reached this can be a good point for a jump or a somersault.

Games and game forms for diving from the pool steps

Diving from the first step
The first dive can be done with the aid of a partner. Bit by bit, this assistance can be dropped off.
Variations:
- Diving in from the second step with and without aid from a partner.
- Diving in from the third step with and without aid from a partner.

Diving with extra tasks

With the aim: "Who can......?" various tasks have to be carried out when diving.
Variations:
- Who can dive the farthest?
- Who can dive the highest?
- Who can make the funniest dive?
- Who can dive over a rope?
- Who can dive into a tire?
- Who can dive through a tire?
- Who can dive and make the biggest splash?
- Who can dive and make the least amount of splash?
- Who can dive over obstacles?

Picking sweets

Who can pick balloons, sweets etc., off a line held up as they jump?

Dolphin dives

Inner tubes that are lying on the surface are used to do dolphin jumps through from the first step of the pool steps.

Variations:
- Doing a dolphin jump from the second step of the pool.
- Doing a dolphin jump from the third step of the pool.
- Doing a dolphin jump through two inner tubes: Jump into the first tube and surface up through the second one.
- Doing a dolphin jump over a pole being held up.

2.3.4 Diving into the Beginners' Pool

Doing simple dives from the edge of the pool

After having done hopping and jumping in the water, diving in from the edge of the pool now provides the beginner with a big step forward.

It is, therefore, recommended that diving like this is first done from a sitting position. For anxious children, assistance would be welcome and this can be reduced methodically bit by bit.

As a general rule, no head first dives are permitted in the beginners' pool.

Diving in from a sitting position from the edge of the pool

Diving in from the edge of the pool begins, first of all, from the edge of the pool with the assistance of a partner. This can be reduced bit by bit.

Variations:
- Diving with the help of a partner: The partner provides assistance by supporting with both hands.
- Diving in from a sitting position with the partner's assistance being reduced bit by bit.
- The partner helps using one hand, then only with his fingers and then only when required for safety.
- Jumping into the partner's arms.
- Jumping or diving without any help.

Diving in from a squatting position on the edge of the pool

Diving in from the edge of the pool is done, first of all from a squatting position with assistance from a partner. This is then slowly reduced bit by bit.

Diving in from a standing position on the edge of the pool
Diving in from the edge of the pool is done, first of all from a standing position with assistance from a partner. Then this is slowly reduced bit by bit.

Diving or jumping in with equipment
When diving or jumping in from the edge of the pool, equipment can be used for the children to orient themselves: Swimming boards, pull buoys, balls, mats, pool noodles etc.
Variations:
• While jumping the children reach out to grab the objects.
• The children jump on to the objects (the objects should not be too close to the edge of the pool).
• The children jump or dive over the objects.

Variations of feet first jumps and dives
Squatting jumps/dives
"Who can lift the legs up into a squat after jumping in?"
    This task can be done in a variety of different ways. Using additional tasks, the basics of twisting in the air (somersault forwards or backwards) can be worked on. These elementary movements can be done by bringing the legs upwards or backwards into a squatting position in the air. When trying these movements out, the swimmers can watch how the upper body is being held.
Variations:
• Who can bring the legs up into a squatting position in front of the body after jumping in?
• Who can bring the legs up into a squatting position under the body after jumping in?
• Who can bring the legs up into a squatting position behind the body after jumping in?
• Who can make their legs small in a squatting position after jumping in?

Jumping steps
Who can do the splits in the air after jumping in?
    Who can make a large step in the air after jumping in?
Variations:
• Who can do a running movement in the air after jumping in?

- Who can do a running movement in the air after jumping in and make the most steps?
- Who can do a slow motion running movement in the air after jumping in?

Jumps with turns about the longitudinal axis
Who can do a half turn about the axis of the body (half screw-turn) in the air after jumping in?
It is recommended that turns in both directions are carried out.
Variations:
- Who can do a full right-handed twist turn in the air after jumping in?
- Who can do a full left-handed twist turn in the air after jumping in?
- Who can do several full twist turns (to the left and to the right) in the air after jumping in?

Jumps with a twist turn in the latitudinal axis
- Who can roll into the water?
- Who can do a roll in the air?
- Who can do a roll in the air and then do a further roll in the water?

Jumps in different directions
Who can jump forwards into the water?
Variations:
- Backwards, sideways etc.
- Who can jump the farthest?
- Who can jump the highest?
- Who can jump the funniest way?
- Who can jump like any kind of animal?
- Who can jump like a frog/dolphin/whale/trout/seal?

For jumping with a partner and a group see Chapters 2.3.6. and 2.3.7.

Diving in from the Edge of the Pool and the 1-m Board 2.3.5

After beginning swimmers have learned to jump in from the edge of the beginner's pool and are in a position to be able to swim, they can be prepared for diving games and exercises in deeper water leading on to diving from the 1-m board.

In this chapter, starting with simple feet first jumps, we introduce popular diving styles. The opportunity to vary the types of feet first jumps leads on naturally to diving with additional tasks. Dives with a partner and in groups round this chapter off.

Popular Diving

By this we mean simple dives one has learned and do not have any particular background. Popular diving is not competitive, rather it is all about having primarily fun when diving. These styles include simple feet first jumps and head dives, falling in like a pack of dominoes, hunched-up jumps, diving in pairs and groups etc. The children should start off by learning popular diving from the edge of the pool and then later move on to learn diving in from the springboard or the high board.

Feet first jumps and variations
Simple feet first jumps
Variations of feet first jumps from the edge of the pool: Squatting jump, stepping jump, split-legged jumps and angled leg jumps, jumps with twist turns in different directions: forwards, backwards, sideways (see Chapter 2.3.4.).

Feet first jumps with additional tasks (see Chapter 2.3.3.)
• Who can jump the farthest?
• Who can jump the highest?
• Who can jump the funniest way?

These simple feet first jumps and their variations can be done starting from the starting blocks and then from the 1-m board and the high board.

Exercise to prepare for the 'domino fall-in'
As a preparatory exercise for getting the body to tense correctly can be done with the following tasks for the 'domino fall-in'.

Rolling into the water sideways
The children lie down on their backs (sides or stomachs) along the edge of the pool and let themselves roll into the water.

Rolling into the water in pairs
The children lie down along the edge of the pool that the child in front can hold on to the legs of the one behind. They now let themselves roll into the water from a position lying on their backs (sides or stomachs).

'Domino fall-in' forwards with a partner
Standing on the edge of the pool, the upper body is bent forwards. The arms are stretched out forwards so that the head is between them. The partner holds the other by his hips to give support to the starting position. The jumper now lifts up onto the tips of his toes and lets himself fall forward into the water. The partner accompanies him at the beginning with the hands.
Variations:
- The help can be reduced bit by bit.
- The fall-in is done from a squatting position.
- The fall-in is done sideways from a standing position.
- The fall-in is done backwards from a standing position.

'Domino fall-in' forwards from the edge of the pool
Standing on the edge of the pool, the upper body is bent forwards. The arms are stretched out forwards so that the head is between them. The jumper now lifts up onto the tips of his toes and lets himself fall forward into the water.
Variations:
- See above.
- The fall-in is done from the 1-m board.

'Domino fall-in' forwards from the 3-m board
Standing on the 3-m board facing the pool, the arms are stretched upwards with the head between them. The jumper now lifts up onto the tips of his toes and lets himself fall forward into the water. The

body is completely stretched out. Let your feet stay in contact to the board, do not jump.
Variations:
- Done first of all with assistance.
- Done sideways from a standing position.
- Done backwards from a standing position.
- Done from the high board.

'Domino fall-in' backwards from the 3-m board or the high board
Standing on the 3-m board with the back to the pool, the arms are stretched upwards with the head between them. The body is fully stretched. The jumper lifts up onto the tips of his toes and lets himself fall backwards into the water. This is again no jump, but a fall where the feed stay in contact with the board as long as possible.

Thrown jump with a somersault in the beginners' pool
One of the partners stands in the beginners' pool to help the other one to do a somersault backwards. The one who jumps holds on to the shoulders of the helping partner und steps into his hands. The helper catapults the jumper into the air, so he can make the somersault backwards.
Variations:
- Thrown jump as a group of three: An additional partner gives assistance.
- A thrown jump somersault forwards.
- A thrown jump somersault with a screw turn.
- Thrown jump somersaults with additional tasks.
    a) As high as possible.
    b) Making a lot of splash.
    c) Making little splash.

'The handle roll'
Two children stand next to each other and place the inner arm akimbo on the hip. One of the children grips the handles and does a forward roll.

Catapult
One person takes another one standing on his shoulders and holds him steady with his hands. The person on the shoulders drops down

into his knees and pushes himself up and off his partner's shoulders into the water.

Variations:

- The partner standing on the shoulders jumps off and does a high jump feet first.
- The partner standing on the shoulders jumps off and does a hunched-up jump.
- The partner standing on the shoulders jumps off and does a flat pike jump forwards (backwards).
- The partner standing on the shoulders jumps off and does a somersault forward.
- Somersault in a group of three: Another person stands by to give assistance.
- Thrown up somersault with a screw twist turn.
- Thrown up somersault with additional tasks - see above.

Head above water

Who can jump off from the edge of the pool with the head dipping into the water?

Variations:

- Jump in from the starting blocks.
- Jump in from the 1-m board.
- Who can jump/dive flat into the water?

Ducks

Who can jump in the water like a duck?

The head and the feet stay on the surface for a long time. The tummy is immersed first of all. This jump can be done to start with from a swimming board or a soft floating mat.

Variations:

- Who can jump in like a duck so that the head stays above water?
- Dive/jump in from the starting blocks.
- Dive/jump in from the 1-m board.
- Who can jump/dive flat into the water?
- Who can splash the most doing the duck?

Hunched up jump

Who can make himself the smallest jumping in?

Picture 10: *Thrown up somersault jumps can be practiced in open water*

The legs can be hunched up under the body and held firmly round the knees.
Variations: See above.

Diving jump
Who is able to jump in from the edge of the pool and dive down to the bottom of it?
Variations: See above.

Feet first jumps and variations
Simple feet first jumps and variations of these jumps can already be learned by non-swimmers in the beginners' pool. Since they have already been covered they are only referred to here: see Chapter 2.3.4.

Jumps and the swimming board
Who can jump over a swimming board?

Variations:
- Who can jump on to one or two swimming boards (watch the distance from the pool's edge).
- Who can jump on to one swimming board and stay on it as long as possible?
- Who can jump over a swimming board and dive under another one?
- Who can jump in between two swimming boards?

Jumping/diving over a rope
Who can jump over a rope?
Variations:
- Who can jump under a rope held up high?
- Who can jump on to a rope and push it under?
- Who can jump in between two ropes?
- Who can jump up in the air and touch a rope held up high with his hand/head?

Jumping/diving and tires
Who can jump into a tire?
Variations:
- Who can jump into one inner tube and surface up through another?
- Who can jump/dive through an inner tube?
- The distance to the inner tube can be increased.
- Who can jump/dive through two inner tubes?
- Who can jump/dive through an inner tube and dive down and bring objects from the bottom (diving rings, 'treasures' etc.)?

Jumps/dives and a mat
Who can jump/dive onto a mat?
Variations:
- Who can jump/dive onto a mat and stay lying on it?
- Who can jump/dive onto a mat and resurface from under the mat?
- Who can jump/dive onto a mat and glide along on it?
- The distance to the mat can be increased.

Jumps/dives with twist turns
Who can demonstrate jumps/dives with twist turns?
Variations:
- Who can do a full right-handed twist turn in the air having jumped/dived in?

- Who can do a full left-handed twist turn in the air after jumping off the ground?
- Who can do more than one full right or left-handed twist turn in the air before diving into the water?

Water bombs
Who can jump that the most water is splashed up?
Variations:
Jump in backwards, jump in sideways, jump in in pairs etc.

Splash free jumping
Who can jump in that the least amount of splash is made?

Theme subjects and jumping/diving
Who can do arithmetic during a jump/dive?
    The instructor shows them various numbers using the fingers on his left and right hands. The jumper/diver has to add these together as he jumps/dives.
Variations:
- The numbers have to be subtracted from each other in the jump/dive.
- The numbers have to be multiplied together in the jump/dive.
- Questions have to be answered as they jump/dive in.

Jumping/diving as a clown
Who can jump/dive in as funny as a clown?

Jumping in and Diving in with a Partner

2.3.6

For children, jumping and diving together with a partner removes any anxiousness they may have and at the same time influences them positively. Doing things together with a partner makes them think of many new ideas on how they can jump/dive in together and how they can execute these movements together.

Games and exercises should, therefore, give special emphasis to these typed of tasks. The children should be given sufficient time to try the various possibilities.

Partner jumping/diving from the edge of the pool
Who can think up ways to jump/dive in with a partner?
Variations:
- Who can do jumps feet first with a partner?
- Who can do funny jumps with a partner?
- Who can do daring jumps with a partner?
- Who can do jumps with a partner on the shoulders?
- et cetera ......

Fantasy jumps/dives
Who can think of ways to do fantasy jumps/dives with a partner?
Variations:
- Doing fantasy jumps/dives in pairs.
- Doing fantasy jumps/dives with several partners.
- Doing fantasy jumps/dives forwards, backwards or sideways.
- Doing fantasy jumps/dives as themes, e.g., magician, fairies, witches, dragons, space travelers etc.

Horse-riding jumps
One of the partners takes the other onto his back and jumps with him into the water.
Variations:
- Who can do a horse-riding jump in with a partner feet first?
- Who can do a horse-riding jump in with a partner head first?
- One of the partners takes the other onto his shoulders and jumps with him into the water.

Handstand jumps/dives
Who can do a handstand with a partner and jump in?
One of the partners can assist with the handstand to start with and then reduce the help later.

The next step for them both to do is the handstand dive together.

Doubles
Who can jump with his partner so one of them jumps/dives in feet first and the other head first at the same time?

Jumping in and Diving in as a Group

Starting out with jumping/diving with a partner, group jumps can now be worked at. At the beginning, the jumps and dives are carried out in small groups and later it can be done in larger groups, too.

All jump in together

All the children stand on the edge of the pool holding hands. Now they all jump into the water together.

Variations:
• Jump in after a command.
• The children let go of their hands after they touch the bottom of the pool with their feet.
• They all try to jump to make as much splash as they can.

Head first as a group

All the children stand on the edge of the pool holding hands. All of them lean forward and then fall head first into the water together.

Variations:
• Jump in after a command.
• The children let go of their hands after they touch the bottom of the pool with their feet.
• All of them try to jump to make as little splash as they can.
• All jump in, one after another like a pack of dominos.

Group bomb

All the children stand next to each other with their backs towards the pool. Each child bends forwards and puts his arms round his neighbor's legs. All of them fall then backwards into the water.

Variations:
• Carry it out forwards.
• Carry it out sideways.

The rolling chain

All the children kneel down one behind the other alongside the edge of the pool, so that they are sideways on to it.

The first child lets itself fall into the water and pulls the other with it.

The mass roll forward
All the children link their arms together and squat down. Then all of them do a roll forward together into the water.

Chain reaction
All the children sit down with their backs to the water as close to the edge as possible. Each of them links the arms with their neighbour. When the first child in the row lets itself fall backwards into the water, then everybody else falls in afterwards.

The bob-sleigh
All the children sit very close to each other on the edge of the pool with one shoulder of each towards the water. Everybody holds on to the shoulders of the one sitting in front. Then the whole group imagines being in a bob-sleigh sliding down the bob-sleigh run. First of all they get into a little curve to the left, so everybody has to lean towards the left side. Afterwards it follows a sharper right curve and all of them lean over to the right side. Finally, they reach a long, very sharp left-hand curve and everybody falls into the water by the time they lean over.

Picture 11: *On the bobsled leaning over*

Artistic Jumping and Diving

This chapter will not cover the traditional forms of artistic jumping and diving, nor the methodical approach to learning the individual jumps and dives themselves. Instead, it covers the game forms, which can be carried out in a playful manner for this area of swimming. However, the method of learning to do a somersault will be shown as an example, whereby this will concentrate more on the game forms that lead up to doing the somersault.

Head first dives
In order to bring children on to learn to do dives head first from the edge of the pool or the springboards, they have to learn, first of all, how to go into the water with their heads leading. This is already taught in beginners' swimming instruction by doing jumps and dives from the steps (see also Volume 1, "Aquafun - Fist Steps", RHEKER 2004).

At this juncture, therefore, the first steps to diving in head first are shown in a short summary.

The gliding dive from the steps
Dive in head first from the steps and then glide on (gliding dive). As this is done, the head is between the arms and the body is fully stretched.
Variations:
- Dive in head first from a squatting position on the first step.
- Dive in head first from a standing position on the first step.
- Dive in head first from the second step.
- Dive in head first from the third step.

Diving through an inner tube head first and then gliding
Variations:
- Dive in over a rope.
- Dive in over a partner's arms.

Diving in head first from a sitting position on the edge of the pool
Variations:
Dive in from a hunched up, squatting position.
Dive in from a standing position.

Diving in head first from one of the starting blocks

Diving in head first from the 1-m board
First of all do a dive head first from a squatting position on the 1-m board.
Variations:
- Do a dive head first from a standing position.
- Take a step forward and then dive in head first.
- Do a dive head first from a walking pace.

The somersault
Preparatory exercises and games leading to learn to do the somersault. The following, methodical steps teach the somersault:

If we beginn with a roll into the water, we have to speed the rolling movement up. The main characteristics of the somersault (tucking the legs up under the body, head down on to the chest, hunching up into a ball etc.,) now can be incorporated. Finally, the somersault forwards can be done from the edge of the pool with help from a partner before you move on in doing it from a higher position (e.g., from the starting block with some help).

Afterwards, the assistance can be slowly reduced. When the children can do the forward somersault from the starting block without any assistance, they are ready to attempt it from the 1-m board.

Forward roll in water
The children have to try to do a forward roll in the beginners' pool
Variations:
- Doing a forward roll with assistance.
- 'The handle roll' (see earlier).
- Who can do two or three forward rolls?
- Do the roll backwards.
- Do a fast forward roll from a standing position.
- Starting with a jump from the standing position, do a fast forward roll.

Picture 12: *Forward roll on the mat in the water as preparation for doing the somersault*

Forward roll into the water
The children get the following task: Who can do a forward roll into the water from a low squatting position from the edge of the pool?
Variations:
- Doing a forward roll with assistance.
- Who can do a forward roll rapidly?
- Tips: Make yourself small, squat down tightly, head on the chest.
- Do a forward roll on a mat that is lying on the water.
- Do the roll backwards.

Games and exercise forms for learning the somersault
- Do a forward roll on a mat that is lying on the water.
- Doing a forward roll rapidly from the tight squatting position.
- The criteria for doing a forward roll rapidly can be practiced: Head on the chest, rapid squatting down movement of the legs

with the ankles touching the bottom; making yourself as small as possible by holding on to the shinbones with the hands.
- Doing a forward roll from a squatting position after a little jump up.
- Doing a forward roll from a standing position with assistance.

The somersault from a standing position with assistance
First of all, two partners assist. They stand by the sides of the jumper and hold him by the shoulder (the partner standing to the left with the left hand) and with the other hand they support the turning movement by holding the lower leg.
Variations:
- One partner helps.
- One partner only supports the turning movement.
- The partner only stands by to help.

Doing a somersault from the starting block with assistance: see above.

Doing a somersault from the starting block without assistance.

Doing a somersault from a standing position from the 1-m board with assistance.

Doing a somersault from a standing position from the 1-m board without assistance.
- From a standing position on the edge of the 1-m board, swing the arms up high and then swing them down to the sides. As this is done the legs bend slightly pressing down onto the board so that it bends slightly down under the pressure. When the board has reached the lowest point of its spring, the legs begin to stretch up (jump off) and the arms swing rapidly upwards. The take-off occurs virtually upwards with the arms remaining stretched upwards. After a short phase in the air and at the top of the jump, the legs are pulled up in a squatting position and the head is placed on the chest. The hands grab hold of the lower legs. In this way a rotation occurs in the forward axis (somersault movement). The rotation is braked by stretching the legs out and lifting the head off the chest. In this way it is possible to dive in

feet first. The signal to 'close' and 'open' can be called out by another person.

Doing a somersault starting with a step forward from the 1-m board.

Doing a somersault from a walking pace from the 1-m board.

Further Artistic Jumps and Dives 2.3.9

After having done simple jumps into the beginners' pool, popular jumps and dives and having learned the basic head first jumps, dives and somersaults, one can talk as a further aim of:
"The children now have to learn to do artistically styled jumps and dives."
We cannot go into all the detail of artistic jumping and diving here. This is because the aim of this book is to cover games and game forms as covered in the previous chapters. Artistic jumps and dives can be covered in the following areas:
• Jumping and diving from the 1-m board.
• Jumping feet first from the 1-m board after a run-up.
• Diving head first.
• Somersault forwards and backwards.
• Dolphin jumps.
• Backwards or reverse somersault (Auerbach).
• Screw/twisting dives.
• Jumps and dives from the 3-m board and the high board.

Funny jumps and dives
Adventurous jumps and dives
Even the first jump from the edge of the beginners' pool demands courage from the children and can be an adventurous experience.
If the jumps and dives are done from a higher point off the ground, then these are combined with even stronger feelings of adventurous experiences and will-power.
When jumping and diving from the springboard, the acceleration gained off the board makes the time in the air longer and this gives a feeling of weightlessness and flexibility in movement e.g., being able to do rotations about the various axes.

By putting on a T-shirt or a neoprene suit, the courage and joy of experimenting is increased so that more daring jumps and dives can be made. By dressing up e.g., at Carnival time, similarly, one's inhibition is overcome to try out daring and creative jumps and dives.

Funny jumps/dives from the 1-m board
Who can do a funny jump/dive?
Variations:
- Funny jumps/dives from the 3-m board.
- Funny jumps/dives in pairs.
- Funny jumps/dives in a group.

Carnival time jumping and diving
At Carnival time or any other event in the year (a sports meeting, a tournament etc.,) the children are allowed to jump/dive in clothed and show off daring and creative jumps/dives.

Jumps/dives with a partner
Who can demonstrate a daring or funny jump/dive with a partner?

Jumping and diving with various pieces of equipment
When jumping and diving from different heights, unusual objects or pieces of equipment can be carried or taken with one.
Variations:
- Jumping in with an umbrella.
- Jumping in with a piece of cloth, which billows out as you come down.
- Jumping with a rope that you try to crack as you jump.
- Jumping in on a bicycle from the high board (see Vol 2 "Aquafun - Games and Fun for the Advanced" RHEKER 2005, p 96).
- Doing a jump in a canoe.
- Jumping variations from different heights.

Jumping like clowns
As a show spot and to loosen up the atmosphere during swimming competitions, clowns can do funny jumps/dives from the diving boards. They can also use unusual equipment such as umbrellas, a bicycle etc.

Picture 13: *New experiences gained jumping with a canoe*

The Impulses for Creative and Playful Training in Life Saving

2.4

"One of the most important ways of moving forward in life is to meet the others half-way."

(unknown)

Introduction

2.4.1

Life saving, is an area of the sport of swimming that is particularly popular with children and youths because of it's social learning.

In a questionnaire about the weighting of the various different areas of swimming instruction, life saving was just as important and popular as games in water. Both were placed far before the learning of techniques and other areas.

The educational aspects of life saving can be classified as follows.

Dare something and be responsible
In life saving, taking responsibility for the others is the main thing. Life savers train to be there for those who get into danger and stand prepared to help them. However, in many situations, courage and will-power are demanded.

Improving one's perception, broadening one's experience of moving
When life saving, one improves the perception of one's own body. This is achieved because the body experiences stress situations and this is balanced by the strain of doing exercise forms for saving people. Similarly, one can assist a partner in difficulties and consciously learn how to deal with such situations.

Better the ability to perceive, extend the experience with movements
When swimming distances underwater, swimming with clothes or doing life saving exercises one learns to be able to assess your own performance and judge it.

Cooperating, being competitive and communicating
Cooperation and communication are essential in life saving. This can be practiced in many of the game forms.
    This aspect also has its own value in competitive situations.

Support one's health, developing a health consciousness
In order to develop an awareness of healthy living, you have to understand the dangers and risks involved, particularly in open waters, and be able to judge these correctly. In this way, you can safely use all the possibilities of being able to exploit the open space available. You can also directly experience the positive effects of swimming and practicing life saving and let this make a contribution to a healthy outlook on life.

That the various educational aspects of the area of life saving can be effected, there are a few movement exercises for life saving introduced at the beginning of the chapter.
    These will materialize in the construction of a varied and happy period of training where games and game forms build the basis of the exercises.

After carrying out some of the games in the free instructional periods, games will be covered for towing, diving, swimming in clothes, games with a lifeline and combined games.

Open Forms of Movement in Life Saving   **2.4.2**

Just as in the other areas of swimming, children (and grown-ups) can also gather a variety of experiences by doing the freely constructed exercises when practicing life saving. Based on the various experiences, they can be combined with a playful form of life saving exercises and developed further.

By using the following movement exercises, life saving can be taught in a playful and varied way:

How can a tired partner be helped along in the water?
Variations:
- Two people help to drag him along.
- He is pushed along.
- He is pulled along.

Moving underwater
What different ways are there to move underwater?
The children experiment how they can dive down to the bottom and move in different ways.
Variations:
- In the main pool, dive down to different depths in different ways.
- Swim a distance underwater in the shortest time possible.
- Swim a distance underwater as slowly as one wants to.
- Swim a distance underwater using flippers.
- Dive through an underwater obstacle course.
- Dive through an underwater obstacle course using different styles: head first, feet first, diagonally, on the tummy, on the back etc.
- Dive together over a distance with a partner.
- Dive wearing life saving clothing and equipment.

Moving fast in water
How can speed be increased in the water?

Variations:
- Running through the water or swimming through it.
- Increasing the stroke frequency.
- Using aids: Flippers, mono-flipper inter alia.
- Pulling a partner with a rope.

Fetching up weights
Who can lift the heaviest weight up out of the water?
Variations:
- Who can bring various diving stones out of different depths?
- Who can bring various diving stones out of different depths using flippers?
- Trying out various techniques.
- Who can bring various diving stones out of different depths with a partner?

The economical way of swimming fully clothed
How can one swim to make rapid movements forward? How can one swim fully clothed and save energy?

Resistance swimming
How can one increase the water resistance when swimming?
Variations:
- Increasing the water resistance swimming in clothes, all-weather trousers etc.
- Increasing the water resistance and swimming speed using aids: Flippers, mono-flipper, clothes etc.
- Swimming with water resistance with a partner.

2.4.3 Towing Games

Towing, one of the basic skills of life saving, can be taught methodically. There is, however, also the possibility to teach it and practice it using games. The following games are suitable for this:

Pulling the partner
Two swimmers pull a third one through the water. The swimmer being pulled is passive and lies quite relaxed on the water.

Variations:
- Changeover after a length.
- The method of pulling can be changed.
  - a) The swimmer being pulled holds onto the shoulders of the other two.
  - b) The swimmer being pulled is lying between the two others is holding on to the shoulders of the first one and lying his feet on the shoulders of the other one.
- A swimmer pulls a partner along on his own.
- The swimmer being pulled along assists by doing leg strokes (the crawl leg stroke or the breast leg stroke).
- The pulling swimmer can wear flippers.
- The distance to be pulled can be changed.
- The pulling swimmer swims with the eyes closed. The swimmer being pulled indicates the direction to go in.
- All the swimmers are wearing life saving clothes and equipment.

Pushing the partner

A swimmer pushes another through the water. The swimmer being pulled is passive and lies quite relaxed on his back on the water.

Variations:
- Changeover after a length.
- The method of pushing can be changed.
  - a) The swimmer being pushed holds on to the shoulders of the other one.
  - b) The swimmer is pushed by his feet.
- The body position is changed.
- Two swimmers push a third one along.
- The distance to be pulled can be changed.
- All the swimmers are wearing life saving clothes and equipment.

Swimming as a pillion rider

One swimmer holds on to the others hips. The partner in front uses the breaststroke arm movements and the one behind does the leg strokes of the breaststroke.

Variations:
- Changeover after a length.
- On a command, the rear partner dives forward under the other and becomes the front swimmer.

- Several couples have a swimming pillion race.
- Groups of three or four swim the pillion stroke.
- The distance to be swum can be changed.
- Change of swimming stroke: Crawl or Backstroke.
- All the swimmers are wearing life saving clothes and equipment.

Saving to the shore
Two swimmers have to get a third one, who stays passive, to the shore (the opposite side of the pool).
Variations:
- Changeover after a length.
- Several groups have a swimming race.
- Two swimmers have to get several people (3-6) to the 'shore'.
- The method of moving the passive partner is changed.
- The distance to be swum can be changed.
- Other variations; see above.

Pulling with the feet
A swimmer lies on his back and lets himself be pulled. He holds his feet up under the other's shoulders.
Variations:
- The method of pulling can be varied.
    a) The pulling swimmer swims the back crawl.
    b) The pulling swimmer swims the backstroke.
    c) The swimmer being pulled assists by using his feet.
- Groups of three or four swim this way.
- The pulling game is done as a relay.
- Other variations; see above.

Butterfly tandem
Two swimmers swim on their stomachs with the rear partner holding on to the one in front. They try to do the butterfly stroke together.
Variations:
- Changeover after a length.
- The pulling swimmer can wear flippers.
- Both swimmers can wear flippers.

- Both swimmers can wear flippers and only do the snaking movements.
- Groups of three or four swim this way.
- The distance to be swum can be changed.

Pulling relay
The techniques of the pulling games above can be used in a relay race.

Pushing relay
The techniques of the pushing games above can be used in a relay race.

Towing
A swimmer holds onto another under the shoulders and tries to pull him along through the water using a leg stroke.
Variations:
- Changeover after a length.
- The method of pulling can be varied.
  - a) The swimmer being pulled is held in an arm lock under the -body.
  - b) The swimmer being pulled is held by the head.
  - c) The swimmer being pulled is held in an arm lock over the body.
- Both swimmers are wearing life saving clothes and equipment when towing.
- The pulling swimmer can wear flippers.
- The distance to be pulled can be changed.
- The distance to be pulled is repeated four times.
- The swimmer being pulled has the eyes closed.
- The swimmer who is pulling has his eyes closed. The swimmer being pulled indicates the direction to go in.

Towing relay races
The techniques of the towing game above can be used in a relay race.
- Changeover between ways of holding the person being pulled.
- All swimmers are wearing life saving clothing and equipment when towing.
- The swimmer pulling can wear flippers.

2.4.4 Underwater Diving Games

Because underwater diving was comprehensively covered in Chapter 2.1, there will only several games and game forms that have not been covered so far be listed at this point. These are games which have primarily to do with the basic techniques of swimming underwater and diving down deep.

Note: The following safety precaution must be observed in all the games and game forms that have to do with swimming underwater and diving deep down.

When swimming under water, each individual must be closely monitored! Cases of hyperventilation must not be allowed.

When diving down under water, each individual must be closely monitored! Cases of hyperventilation must not be allowed.

Gliding underwater
After diving in from the edge of the pool, who can glide the furthest?
Variations:
• After diving in, who can glide the furthest without using the arms or legs?
• After diving in, who can glide the furthest by using one stroke of the arms?
• After diving in, who can dive deep down by breathing out and reach then a diving ring which is lying under water?
• Who can, having thrown a diving ring into the water and diving in after it, reach it before it sinks to the bottom of the pool?

Swimming underwater
Who can swim 10m underwater?
Variations:
• Extend the length to be swum (15-50m).
• Who can pick up diving rings when swimming underwater?
• Who can pick up the most rings, which have been distributed round in a 10m broad stretch of a swimming pool length?
• Swimming underwater using different techniques: Swimming underwater using a breaststroke arm movement, a mix of the breaststroke arm movement and the leg movements of the crawl, only using the crawl leg movements etc.

- Wearing life saving clothing and equipment when swimming underwater.
- Using flippers.
- Swimming underwater and twisting and turning about the axis of the body.
- Who can swim a certain distance (e.g., 25m) by using the least number of arm strokes?
- Who can swim a distance underwater in the shortest time?

Swimming underwater through a slalom
Who can swim underwater through a marked slalom course in the fastest time?
Variations: see above.

Swimming underwater through 'gates'
Several 'gates' (tires with weights) are set in a lane underwater. Who can dive through the 'gates' without coming up for breath?
Variations: see above.

Swimming blind underwater
Who can swim under water for a laid down stretch blindfolded?
Variations: see above.

Diving down feet first
Who can dive to the bottom at a depth of 2-3m feet first?
Variations:
- Increase the depth to be dived.
- When diving deep down, who can pick up diving rings and bring them up to the surface?
- Who can pick up the most rings?
- Who can bring the heaviest weight up to the surface?
- When diving wear life saving clothes and equipment.
- Who can collect the diving rings in the shortest time?

Diving down head first
Who can dive to the bottom at a depth of 2-3m head first?
Variations:
- Try out various ways of diving.
- Dive with flippers.

- Who can pick up a submerged dummy, surface it and tow it along?
- Who can collect up the submerged objects in the shortest time?
- Further variations see above.

Swimming underwater relay races
- see Chapter 2.1 "Impulses for Creative and Playful Diving".

Combinations of swimming underwater and diving down into the depths
Who can swim for 10m underwater and then dive down to a depth of 3m to fetch an object?
Variations:
- The distance to be swum underwater can be increased.
- Increase the depth to be dived to.
- Further variations see above.

2.4.5 Swimming in Clothes

Swimming in clothes is not only important for life saving training. Children, who think they are OK as swimmers because they have their first swimming badge, often forget their swimming ability when they fall into water in clothes.

Therefore, swimming in clothes (T-shirt, pajamas/nightdress and other articles of clothing) should be included in every swimming lesson.

Swimming a stretch in clothes
Who can swim one lane of the pool in life saving clothes (jacket and pants)?
Variations:
- Swimming a lane dressed only in the jacket.
- Swimming a lane dressed only in the pants.
- Swimming dressed in the jacket and pants.
- After swimming a bit the jacket and pants are taken off in the water.
- The distance to be swum can be increased.
- The distance to be swum can be done in using different techniques: Breaststroke, crawl, backstroke.

- Swim in different positions (on the stomach, on the side, on the back).
- Swimming with different breathing frequencies.
- Swimming with handicaps: Eyes closed etc.

Swimming in clothes against the clock

Who can swim a set distance (a length or 200m) in life saving clothes (jacket and pants) in a certain time?

Variations:
- Who can swim the longest distance in 10 minutes?
- Each time the set distance is swum again, it has to be done in a faster time.
- Further variations see above.

Swimming in clothes with flippers

Who can swim a length in life saving clothes (jacket and pants) wearing flippers?

Variations: see above.

Swimming in clothes and diving down

Who can swim a length of the pool in life saving clothes (jacket and pants) and dive down once and touch the bottom?

Variations:
- Diving to touch the bottom is done 2-4 times in a length.
- When diving down, objects have to be brought to the surface.
- The length to be swum can be extended.
- The distance to be swum can be done using different techniques: Breaststroke, crawl, backstroke.
- Swim in different positions (on the stomach, on the side, on the back).
- Swimming with different breathing frequencies.
- Swimming with handicaps: Eyes closed etc.
- Further variations see above.

2.4.6 Games with a Rope

Throwing a life saving ring
Who can throw a life saving ring or life saving float to a neighbor who is swimming in the water?
Variations:
- Who can throw a life saving ring or life saving float the most accurately into a target area?
- There are several couples swimming in the water. Who can throw a life saving ring or life saving float to the person swimming the farthest away?

Pulling the partner back to 'dry land'
A swimmer, who is 10m away from the edge of the pool, is pulled back to 'dry land' by his partner.
Variations:
- Two pairs, each pull a partner to the edge of the pool. Which pair can do it the fastest?
- A life saver has to pull several swimmers back to the edge of the pool.
- Several partners are pulled back to 'dry land' in a relay race.

Throwing a life saving ring and pulling a partner to the edge
Who can throw a life saving ring or life saving float to the nearest neighbor who is swimming in the water, and pull him as quickly as possible back to land?
Variations:
- Two or more pairs compete against each other. Which couple is the fastest?
- A life saver has to pull several swimmers back to the edge of the pool.
- Several partners are pulled back to 'dry land' in a relay race.

Combined Games

Note: The following safety precautions must be observed in all the games and game forms to do with swimming underwater and diving deep down.

When swimming underwater and diving down underwater, each individual must be closely monitored! Cases of hyperventilation must not be allowed.

Swimming and avoiding hitting things

In the main pool, several objects are distributed about (swimming boards, pull buoys, airbeds, pool noodles etc.).

Who can swim a length of the pool avoiding these obstacles? If any obstacle or another swimmer is touched, the swimmer has to start again.

Variations:

- The distance to be swum can be done using different techniques: Breaststroke, crawl, backstroke.
- The length to be swum can be extended (2 or more lengths).
- Swim in different positions (on the stomach, on the side, on the back).
- Swimming with different breathing frequencies.
- Swimming with different handicaps: Eyes closed, a partner gives indications from the side of the pool.
- Two swimmers form a tandem and swim together round the obstacles.

Combination of swimming underwater and diving down

Who can swim for 10m underwater and then dive down to a depth of 3m to fetch up an object?

Variations:

- The distance to be swum underwater can be increased
- Increase the depth to be dived to.
- Who can dive down and collect diving rings and bring them to the surface?
- Who can pick up the most rings?
- Who can bring the heaviest weight up to the surface?
- When diving wear life saving clothes and equipment.

- Dive down wearing flippers.
- Who can pick up a submerged dummy, surface it and tow it along?

Combination of swimming and diving down
Who can swim 20m and then dive down to a depth of 3m to collect an object?
Variations:
- The distance to be swum can be extended.
- The swimming technique can be alternated: Crawl, backstroke or breaststroke.
- Further variations see above.

Combination of pushing and pulling exercises
One partner tows another down one one lane and then changes over to push him along.
Variations:
- After completing half a length - changeover.
- The way of pulling is varied:
- Changeover between pulling and pushing.
- Changeover between the underarm grip and pushing.
- Changeover between the underarm grip and pulling.
- Changeover between the underarm grip and the locked arm grip.
- Changeover between the underarm grip and the head grip.

Combined exercises with diving and towing
Two swimmers swim along - one on the surface and one underwater immediately below the one on the surface. After swimming about 10m using the crawl, a 5kg ring is brought up from the bottom of the pool by swimmer No 1. The other swimmer (No 2 on the surface) carries out a freeing movement after being grappled by swimmer No 1 after he has dropped the 5kg ring to the bottom and is then pulled back to the nearest edge of the pool by swimmer No 2 using the underarm grip.
Variations:
- The distance to be swum can be shortened or lengthened.
- The breaststroke is used.
- Swimmer No 1 changes the role with swimmer No 2.
- Both swimmers start with a dive from the 3-m board.
- The head grip is used for towing.
- The exercise is carried out in clothing (T-shirt, life saving clothing).

Towing the diving ring
A 5-kg diving ring is brought up from the bottom of the pool and is then towed 15m using the backstroke.
Variations:
- Towing using a stomach lying position.
- Towing using a sideways lying position.
- Doing the exercise as a relay.
- Laying the diving ring on the chest and using the backstroke.
- Dive down and collect the diving ring having swum a distance to get to it and then tow it back.

The Impulses for Creative and Playful Artistic and Synchronized Swimming 2.5

"A harvest is always the fruits of patience"

Gordan PAULUSZ

Introduction 2.5.1

In particular, it is the creative games involving movement to music that encapsulate the area of artistic and synchronized swimming with its variety of interpretation.

These creative and imaginative activities in the environment of water can be covered in various ways and combined with the following pedagogic aspects.

In this the terms of the *shaping of movements* and *expression* take on a particular meaning:

Expressing oneself using the body, making movements
Coming from the little games in the beginners' pool right up through to artistic and synchronized swimming, movements can be made to be creative and inventive.

When doing them, one can carry them out as an individual or in a group very expressively and creatively and present very impressive movements.

Improving one's perception, broadening one's experience of moving
When doing artistic and synchronized swimming, the perception of one's own body is experienced anew and improved by the fact that by moving in the space the body is experienced differently.

The possibilities of being able to move the body are broadened by learning new movement sequences such as e.g., moving rhythmically in water, being able to construct different lines through the water as one moves etc.

Experiencing one's capability, understanding it and being able to judge it
When choreographing the elements of movement (whether it is with the smallest, simple elements done in the beginners' pool or those in artistic and synchronized swimming) and then demonstrating the results, one can assess one's own capability and judge it. Similarly, this can be done in a group.

Cooperating, being competitive and communicating
Cooperation and communication are particularly demanded when carrying out group tasks and practicing the structure of free exercises.

Furthering one's health, developing a health consciousness
Health consciousness can be developed by using specific exercises which support stamina and concentration.

2.5.2 The Forms of Movement for Artistic and Synchronized Swimming

The forms of movement for artistic and synchronized swimming, that are freely constructed, allow children (and grown-ups) to collect various new experiences on how they are able to construct imaginative and impressive movements. Finding out these factors by themselves helps to develop creativity in children and makes sure that they are fully motivated to take part in the exercises (intrinsic motivation).

The following movement exercises help to acquire the artistic and synchronized swimming:

Doing movements to music
Some rhythmical music is being played. Each child moves in time to the rhythm of this music in the beginners' pool. After a session of trying things out, some of the children are allowed to show off what they have created, with the aim of giving the others' ideas as food for thought.
Variations:
- Two children create a series of movements agreeing with each other what to do.
- Three or four children create a series of movements agreeing with each other what to do.
- Several children create a series of movements agreeing with each other what to do.

Doing movements to music in a group
Groups of four to six children are formed. Some rhythmical music is played and each group has to think of ways of moving to the music in the beginners' pool.

After a period of trying things out, some of the groups are selected to demonstrate what they have created.
Variations:
- The groups are formed differently.
- The best sequences from each of the groups are chosen to be combined to build a free exercise sequence.

Building figures
Groups of 4-8 children get together. Some rhythmical music is played and each group tries to build a figure to the music from the members of the group.
Variations:
- The groups are formed differently.
- The figure that they have to build is laid down beforehand e.g., geometric figures: circle, square, trapezium etc.
- They can also form normal everyday objects as a figure: Toaster, windmill, car, submarine etc.
- They can also form things from nature, from art or politics, from space etc.

Play-acting
The groups have to carry out the following movements: Try to act out everyday scenes from life in a moving presentation.
Variations:
- Act out nursery rhymes in a moving presentation.
- Act out historical moments in a moving presentation e.g., famous battles (such as the Battle of Bunker Hill), the Boston Tea Party etc.
- Act out various kinds of sports in a moving presentation.
- Depict well-known monuments (e.g., Statue of Liberty) in a moving presentation.

Acting out animals
Groups of 4-8 children get together. Each group has to try to act out an animal or family of animals.

Acting out the news
Groups are formed. They have to try to represent parts of a news broadcast e.g., the weather report, sports news, political news etc.

Making up games
The groups are given various pieces of equipment, which they have to use to make up a game with its own rules by experimenting with the equipment.

Equipment that can be made available for this game could be pool noodles, swimming boards and light balls. A possible game could be:

They can 'bat' the ball between them by using the swimming boards. After a specific number of contacts with the ball, it is played through a pool noodle which is held up high as a basketball basket. If the swimming boards are off different colors then these 'colors' can play against each other.

2.5.3 Game Forms in the Beginners' Pool

Creative movement games
Mirror
Two persons stand in front of each other about 1-2m apart.

One of the partners now has to do a mirror image movement to that done by the other person.

Contrast dancing

Two persons stand in front of each other like in the game of Mirror.

One of the partners now has to do the opposite movement that the other person does.

Representing animals

By doing different forward movements try to mimic an animal. The other children have to try and guess which animal is being represented.

Variations:

- Different animals have to be represented: Frogs, elephants, storks etc.
- Two or three children have to represent the animal together.

Icicles

1-3 catchers represent 'winter'. Anybody they touch 'freezes' like an icicle. That person can be set free again when two people who are not yet caught put their arms around him.

The master/mistress and his/her dog

Two children move next to each other around the beginners' pool. Partner A tries to keep alongside Partner B and imitates all the movements and changes of direction Partner B makes.

Variations:

- Go in different directions: Forwards, backwards or sideways.
- Use different methods of forward movement: Running, hopping, jumping etc.
- Use diving, gliding, handstand and other tricks.

Floating log

The children form a corridor. At the beginning of the corridor, one of the children floats on the water and is pushed along this corridor.

Games to Music   2.5.4

Bingo

All the children join hands and swim around in a circle singing the 'Bingo' song (or dance round in the beginners' pool:

"A weenie little puppy, a weenie little puppy
Was sitting on the window-sill all a-floppy
(all swim round in a circle to the right)
A weenie little puppy, a weenie little puppy
Was sitting on the window-sill all a-floppy
(swim in a circle now to the left)
Bee / I / eN / Gee / Oh (three times)
Bingo was his name
(all thrust themselves up above the water)
Bee / I / eN / Gee / Oh
(all swim together to the middle swinging their arms up high together)"

Dancing with balloons

Each child has a balloon and moves around with it in the water. One game could be: Try to keep the balloon up in the air so that it doesn't touch the water.
Variations:
- Using different parts of the body to bounce the balloon up into the air.
- Swapping the balloon with other children.
- Pushing the ball over the water with the head.

Dancing down the path

All the children form a corridor path in the beginners' pool. A child (or a pair) dances down the path to lively music. The children forming the corridor pick up the movements of the dancer(s) and imitate them.

Further games to music: "Dance of the magnets", "Dancing opposites", "Animal movements to music", "Ring a Ring o' Roses", "Up I stretch".

Copy-cat swimming

Everyone chooses a partner. One of them moves around the beginners' pool in as many different ways of moving as he can think of. The other partner copies him as closely as possible. After 2-3 minutes the roles change over.

Variations:
- The pair moves on different paths through the pool.
- One of the partners employs different ways of moving through the water.
- The paths through the pool, speed and method are varied.
- The movements are done to music.
- The game is played in the main pool.
- Movements are also done underwater.

2.5.5

Game Forms for Figure Swimming in the Pool

Synchronized swimming in a group
A group of 3-6 people try to swim alongside each other, synchronizing their movements with each other.
Variations:
- Using different swimming stroke styles.
- Using combinations of different strokes.
- Which group is synchronized the best?
- Which group is the most creative in their synchronization?

Copy-cat swimming
One swimmer in a pair swims using a creative swimming style. The other partner watches him and tries to copy the movements.
Variations:
- They swim different swimming stroke styles.
- They swim using combinations of different strokes or swim using individually created styles.
- They swim round different paths.
- They swim using different techniques and speeds.

Swimming copying figures
One of the partners draws a figure on a piece of paper or makes the shape with his finger in the air. The other partner tries to copy the figure.
Variations:
- The figure has to be swum using different strokes.

- Different segments of the figure are done using different swimming techniques.
- The swimmer chooses different routes when swimming and swims in different patterns.
- Swimming above and underwater are combined (three-dimensional).

Partner swimming
Two partners join one hand and swim the crawl together.
Variations:
- The partners do the same exercise with the breaststroke.
- They swim using different swimming techniques.
- The swimmers choose different routes when swimming and swim in different patterns.
- Swimming above and underwater are combined.

Creative swimming
Each swimmer tries to swim the most imaginatively, creatively or beautifully.
Variations:
- Each one swims, trying to be the funniest.
- Each one swims, moving in the different creative styles.

Creativity relay race
Each member in the relay race team tries to swim in the most imaginative, creative or beautiful style. Each one has to demonstrate a different creative swimming technique. Speed is not the main thing though, as this is the originality shown. The team that wins is the one that has demonstrated the most different and imaginative swimming style.
Variations:
- The winner is the team that is the funniest.
- Creative swimming techniques can be done by groups of pairs.

Rotation swimming
When swimming the crawl try to do a sideways twist through 180° between each full stroke.
Variations:
- Try to do the rotation after each half stroke.
- Doing rotation swimming as a relay race.

Swimming feet first
Who can swim leading with the feet first?
Variations:
- Swimming a relay race feet first.
- Trying out different techniques.

Rhythmical swimming
The swimmers try to swim rhythmically to music, individually or in groups.
Variations:
- Moving to different kinds of music.
- Trying out different techniques.
- Swimming along different paths.
- Which group can swim the best synchronization?

Games and Game Forms for Pattern Swimming 2.5.6

Swimming patterns is an early form of artistic and synchronized swimming. These traditional patterns are ideal for leading up to artistic and synchronized swimming. Some of these patterns are shown in the following section.

Geometrical figures
The following geometrical forms can be used as patterns: Square, circle, oval, rectangle, triangle etc.

Creative patterns
Groups of 6-12 people are asked to make up their own figures and patterns.

Doing predetermined patterns
Using the examples in Diagram 1 (page 169), groups of 6-12 people have to swim the set patterns.

2.5.7 **Games and Game Forms for Artistic and Synchronized Swimming**

Flower petals

Two swimmers lie in the water on their backs with their feet touching each other. Each flips over backwards like a dolphin and does an inwards wheel underwater. Just before they resurface facing each other with their hands touching. As they surface they push the hands up opening just like the petals on a flower.

The star

The group members (6 people) try to form the outline of a star on the water.

Variations:

- 4-8 people try to form the outline of a star on the water.
- Form a star with the feet touching.
- Form a star with the hands touching.
- The star enlarges and shrinks by the swimmers swimming away from each other and then coming together again.
- Which group can form the largest star?
- Which group can form the smallest star?
- Which group can form the largest three-dimensional star where parts of the body are sticking up out of the water (arm, knee, leg etc.).

The wheel

The group members (2-4 people) try to form the outline of a wheel on the water. First of all they form a long row where the feet of the person behind each one is resting against the shoulders of the one in front of him. The leading person now dives down head first under the water and swims to form a wheel underwater. The others follow the same route without losing contact with each other.

Variations:

- 4-8 people try to form the wheel in the water.
- Which group can form the largest wheel?
- Which group can 'keep the wheel rolling' the longest?

Combinations of different patterns

The group members (6-8 people) try, first of all, to form the outline of a star on the water and then go on to make other patterns.

Variations:

- Increase the numbers in the group.
- Vary the sequence of the patterns.
- Build in sequences requiring lifting up out of the water.

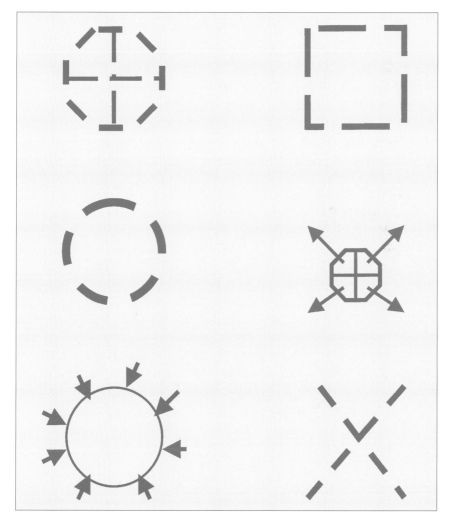

Diagram 1: *Suggestions for patterns to be copied*

2.6 The Impulses for Creative and Playful Aqua Fitness (F. DUNSCHEN)

"It takes effort and pain to help yourself,
but the joy has to be shared with others."

(freely translated from HENRIK IBSEN)

2.6.1 Introduction

The forms of movement that stem from aqua fitness contribute a lot towards ensuring a variety in the broad spectrum of games in water for beginners and advanced participants. They also bring in fresh aspects for moving about in water. Even grown-ups of different constitutions and different age, whose instinct to play may have been lost in the course of their lives, can be encouraged to move in water again.

Aqua fitness, compared to the general form of fitness training, has become by far more interesting. There are numerous similarities to the ways of moving on dry land, but the main difference is that the movements now take place in water.

The term 'aqua fitness' encompasses accordingly a variety of movement forms. In detail it covers:

- *'Aqua aerobics'* with a main emphasis on the development of fitness and the ability to coordinate.
- *'Aqua power'* with emphasis on strengthening exercises and stamina training.
- *'Aqua jogging'* as the main element for stamina training.
- *'Aqua gymnastics'* as the main element for movement training.
- *'Aqua "wellness"* [1] with the main emphasis on relaxation and feeling well.

---

1 Definition: "Wellness" (U.S.) mental and physical soundness: physical well being, especially when maintained or achieved through good diet an regular exercise.

The individual terms, and therefore their content, are often not clearly separate from each other. It is established that there is a different weighting of motives which are having fun or the improvement of the general well-being of the individual, improvement of general stamina, flexibility and the ability to coordinate as well as to improve strength. Combinations of the various spheres are also normal and make sense. Aqua fitness differs from the sport of swimming in that the body is held up vertically in the water. The aim is usually the movement by itself rather than being able to cover a stretch in a quick time with a perfect technique. The upright position of the body with the head above water permits conversation during the training and allows the training and game forms to be conducted better with the addition of verbal communication.

Aspects such as having fun, socializing and relaxation are primary factors for many of the participants in aqua fitness training. Ambitious sportsmen and women follow parts of the aim in their training plan, for example recovering after a competition, specifically recuperating after an injury or copying some of the individual targets from their training sessions in the water. The practically isokinetic training conditions in water offer a whole variety of applications.

The different areas of aqua fitness must in no way be seen as being isolated from each other. It is more the mixed forms, where individual preferences can be pursued, that are more common. Regarding the use of music or equipment and the size of groups, it is possible to be quite varied in the methods chosen. Creativity in the session is, therefore by no means, foreign.

The features that have been described permit the mixture of a colorful palette towards the aim i.e., the contents can be well matched to meet the most varied prerequisites of the participants. In heterogeneous groups, with trained and untrained people in them, old/young and swimmers as well as non-swimmers, and whose members should at least be used to water, there is the opportunity for each of them to be able to match his level of training to the demands and achieve appropriate improvements.

The numerous positive effects of running movements, which can be copied in water, can only receive a passing mention here: The weightlessness in water leads on amongst other things to a feeling of well-being and permits stamina training, strength training and flexibility to be exercised with little stress or strain on the joints of the body. The coldness of water to the body increases the resistance of the body and increases the burning off of energy. The feeling of water passing over the skin has a massaging effect and at the same time increases the circulation in the body. The requirement to keep the body upright gives a constant stimulus to keep and exercise a perfect balance.

The principles of the training have to be sufficiently observed, however, these should still lie within the panoply of being taught in a playful manner.

2.6.2 Aqua Jogging

*"Even a journey of a thousand miles
begins with a simple first step."*

Japanese proverb

After giving a short description of the methods of the running techniques, some games with running movements in both shallow and deep water will be covered. The examples of the games covered show that, with a little fantasy, dry land games can be adapted for use in water.

Equipment
Running in water can, in principle, be carried out without any requirement for floatation aids. This is dependent, amongst other things, on the make up of the texture of the body and the level of training and is generally strenuous. When running in deep water, it is a question of keeping afloat and often only achievable by adding the occasional swimming movement to assist. It is therefore recommended that a flotation aid be used that doesn't restrict the breathing and doesn't impede the use of the arms.

The flotation aids have to be fitted in the area of the center of gravity of the body. These flotation aids *(e.g., 'Aquajogger', Speedo-*

Belt) can be bought for about $20 upwards. With a little ingenuity, usable flotation aids can be homemade and tried out. Experiments with self-made flotation aids have the advantage of teaching one which the best material is to use and where the center of gravity is. The physical laws of flotation of bodies in water can thus be learned in a practical way and the exercise does away with calculating formulae.

Running techniques

In shallow water, like in the beginners' pool, the running movements used on dry land can be applied in water. The resistance of the water reduces the speed of movement considerably. First of all, the slowed down movements limit you being able to take steps to swerve round things. At the beginning, this leads to trying to go too fast or use too much energy.

In deep water, the flotation aids ensure that the head stays above the surface of the water without having to strain oneself. When the flotation aids are fitted in *the area of the center of gravity of the body. This permits various different ways of holding the body*. It is easier to keep an upright position if these are fitted like a belt round the body in the area of the belly button.

The running techniques are no different from normal ones and therefore can be copied quite easily. The water resistance and the lack of contact with the ground create initially a peculiar feeling.

There are four particular running movements that have the following characteristics:

Walking pace: This movement is similar to the normal movement of routine walking. The water resistance is felt mainly on the lower leg because of the way it is moved. The most important part of the movement is the way that the lower leg is swung deliberately forwards in a sort of kicking motion. As the lower leg swings forward the knee is lifted slightly. As it swings back it passes underneath the center of the body axis to the rear. The step frequency should be - dependent on the state of training - about 25-30 paces a minute for beginners.

The stride: The important feature here is the stretch forwards and backwards of the whole of the leg. After the knee has been lifted up almost as high as a horizontal position, the lower leg is swung forwards. Following this the leg is stretched to the rear as far as possible. Because the stride requires more effort than the walking pace, it is not so suitable for long periods of stamina training.

Knee-lifting style: Lifting the knee and stretching the leg are the most significant characteristics of this style. The features of the knee-lifting style; the knees are lifted alternately up to at least the horizontal position at a high frequency followed by a distinct stretch of the legs to the rear. The knee-lifting style is quite suitable for fast moving games, because of the high step frequency and its variability. According to the direction of movement, the water resistance is felt on the knee and the sole of the foot. The movement of the legs is similar to the feeling when climbing stairs.

"Robo-Jog": This is running like a robot with relatively little movement in the knee joints. The legs are stretched out fully in the forward and rearward movement. As a result there is relatively a lot of water resistance created, thus permitting only a slow pace frequency.

One must think clearly how to move so that lasting strain, caused by habitual wrong movements, can be prevented. It is therefore necessary, to use the movements in games, to teach the correct way to execute them as well as to induce the correct way of thinking regarding these running methods. A healthy way of moving must be learned, and where it needs to be, use separate exercises that allow corrections. Dependent on how the groups of participants are put together, the game element can be made harder with a parallel increase of adequate execution of the movements.

The construction of the individual exercise periods can - together with a lasting challenging character - be brought together into a single concept. This requires a certain degree of fine feeling from the trainer/exercise leader. Each lesson must have at least a warm-up phase, a main element and a cooling-down period, with all phases being done in a playful manner: Games with limited intensity and stretching exercises are done at the beginning, an intensive game is played in the main element, and then, for example, relaxation exercises or gentle games round off the lesson.

The exertion in the game forms and the training effects or adaptations that they provoke can often be compared with the effects of interval training. In order to control the effects of these exertions, besides a general method of observing the participants, the use of measuring heart rates is recommended. A small portable pulse meter equipment can be used to give the participants a quick view of their pulse rate. Generally, this makes them think more about the function of their bodies and the good use of movement as a means towards maintaining a healthy lifestyle. The measurement of the heart rate using the finger and thumb method is also suitable but it is not so accurate. This involves measuring the pulse rate of the neck (carotid) artery (medical advice should be sought on this) or the wrist for 10 seconds and then multiplying the result by a factor of 6. The group must learn all this before they can read any value into it.

The frequency of steps in the running movements in water is generally the deciding factor for a change of heart rate. Dependent on the training condition of each person, this is individually different. The heart rate, however, is also affected by other physical factors such as a feeling of well being in the water. The demands on the participants have to be measured out appropriately in doses (e.g., using intensive and less intensive games).

The best defense against overloading is always a question of having an understanding of ones own capabilities and being able to recognize this. The measures already mentioned encourage the development of an understanding of the overloading problem and allow one to act accordingly.

Controlling the overload rate, within a game, is not something that the exercise leader can often do because of the dynamics of the game situations themselves. The character of a game suffers by introducing too many breaks in play. Therefore, in order to control the overload situation, the selection of a particular game is what matters. It is also possible to play an intensive game in a less exerting manner as per suggestions from the participants. Once the participants have a good feeling for a certain game, they should always have the possibility of having their say on how the situation can be controlled.

2.6.3 Game Suggestions for Aqua Fitness

The games have been listed in order of complexity with complex games following the more simple ones. Because of the inclusion of variations, however, the demands can be slightly mixed up regarding the stamina and the coordination required and this fact should be noted accordingly.

In groups that have only just been formed, it is recommended that games in which one gets to know the others are played where the technical coordination and the physical demands lie in the lower levels.

Remembering names

The group is standing in a circle in the beginners' pool or in the main pool using the Aquajogger equipment. The first person passes a ball to any other person in the group, who calls out his/her name and looks at the next person to whom he/she will pass the ball. The ball is then passed on and the person then crosses his/her arms to show that he/she may not be passed to again in that round of the game.

Everyone must note to whom they have passed the ball. If everyone has received the ball then the game is repeated in the same order of passing. This time, however, the person passing the ball has to call out the name of the person he/she is passing to. The speed of passing the ball can be increased. Cooperation and communication becomes very important, particularly the business of looking at the next person before passing the ball on.

Variations:
- An additional ball is passed round clockwise.
- A third ball is passed around counterclockwise.
- A different order of passing is worked up and four balls or objects are used.

The molecular game

All the players run through the water with music in the beginners' pool. When the music stops, the exercise leader calls out a number, the players have to form groups of this number and carry out a movement task (e.g., only three feet from all the participants may be touching the bottom, or which group can cover the largest or smallest area?)

Variations:

- Everyone does aqua jogging round the main pool. When the music stops they form different sized groups and execute simple set patterns from artistic swimming.
- Various parts of the body may not touch the water.
- Lift up a member of the group out of the water etc.

Copy-cat

All the participants do aqua jogging e.g., with different step styles in pairs, one behind the other. The leader in the pair varies the movements all the time while the other person tries to imitate the movements in time and as accurately as possible i.e., shadowing him.

Passing the swimming board

The group forms a circle in the beginners' pool. A swimming board is passed round the circle.

Variations:

- The swimming board is passed round under the surface of the water.
- Everyone puts one foot on his swimming board. Each person now tries to change the position in the group without losing the swimming board.
- Weights e.g., diving rings or other objects are passed round.

Picture 14: *Passing the ball overhead*

Passing the ball

The group forms a circle in the water. A ball is passed backwards over the head.

Variations:

- Weights e.g., diving rings or other objects are passed round.
- Before passing the ball, the player has to sink down in the water, submerging his head.
- The object is passed on using one hand.

Winter sales

The participants are placed in equal sized groups or in family groups of up to five members (variable). On the poolside, each group is allotted a '*house*' (e.g., an inner tube) equidistant as far as possible from the center of the pool. In the center of the pool is the '*Supermarket*' (e.g., a mat fixed in position) that has about five sets of different colored balls (i.e., 5 red balls, 5 blue balls etc., or other objects which are all the same). The different colored balls are '*reserved goods*' that have to be carried back to the families in their '*houses*'. Each family may send only one member to collect the purchases and he may collect only one of the '*goods*' at a time. However, the purchaser may not only collect his own 'goods', he can also collect other families' '*goods*'. 'Goods' already collected at home can also be taken from other families' 'houses' unhindered.

The family that wins is the one that has managed to collect all the 'reserved goods' for that family in their 'house'.

Note: The game develops more easily than often imagined beforehand. The playing time is relatively short and forecasts of which family will win are hardly possible. The development of strategic moves make the game more interesting.

Variations:

- Change the style of running.
- Two members in each group join hands and go shopping together.
- The purchased items are particularly heavy or large.
- The 'goods' that have been deposited in the families' houses are taboo.
- Other families making purchases may not be hindered.

Relay race
Run relay races with different running styles.
Variations:
- A carrying race.
- Pushing or pulling relay races.
- Relay races combined with throwing at targets with penalty runs for misses etc.

Further games
"Chain catch", "Fisherman, Fisherman - How deep is the Water?", "The Ten Pass game", "Water basketball" etc.

Aqua Wellness (U.RHEKER) 2.6.4

Aqua wellness is a new form of the area of aqua fitness, and which can be principally associated with relaxation and well being in water.

The importance of relaxation for stressed fellow citizens is ever on the increase in our society of peak performance. This is why there are many forms of relaxation training that are on offer from various sources (evening classes, fitness centers etc.). Relaxation can be found more and more in the environment of water. Therefore, this is why aqua wellness is introduced here.

What does one want to achieve with aqua wellness?

One of the aims of aqua wellness is to use relaxation to increase the ability to perform or regain it. This ability is dependent on different factors and can be shown in an exponential curve.

In order to be able to perform well, the level of activation must be brought onto a normal level e.g., hyperactive children have to be calmed down whereas hypoactive children must be spurred on. Stressed people have to be brought back from their over-exaggerated level so that this can become more effective in their abilities. This occurs using forms of relaxation.

Forms of relaxation
First of all, it will be explained what forms of relaxation are available and how they are effective.

In order to be able to perform correctly, their level of activation has to be returned to normal.

The inner state of tension and the emotional state that are for example very high where hyperactivity is present are brought down to a medium level by triggering a tenseness in the peripheral area i.e., by creating muscular tension in the form of a contraction or a stretching of the muscle or by creating a long-term load on the cardiovascular system etc.

There are active and passive forms of relaxation.

Passive recuperation

Included in passive recuperation are short-term rests by adopting positions of relaxation (lying on the back, lying on the stomach, hocking down, balancing positions) and sleeping.

After exertions in swimming, one can relax by hanging on to the side of the pool or floating motionless in the water, with or without aids such as swimming boards, aqua noodles or the aqua jogging belt.

Active recuperation

Active recuperation means creating psycho-physical relaxing situations by carrying out alternative activities. This can be achieved by changing the load or its form e.g., after a very mentally demanding activity there follows a physical demand on the body - a static load is alternated by a dynamic load etc.

Basic principle: The alternative activity that follows must possess a less demanding intensity.

Forms of psycho-physical regulation

There are several different forms of psycho-physical regulation:

1. Short-term intense, general physical loading

The organism is loaded very intensely for a short period, alternating between passive and active recuperation designed to create psychological release and physical fatigue.

A considerable problem in this is the dosage: Where a wrong application of the dosage has occurred this is followed by a slight overshoot of the reactions.

Examples of exercises suitable for intensive games of movement are e.g., running and catching games, strengthening games and games of skill inter alia.

Running and catching games
Fighter jet - Sailplane
When the words "Fighter jet" are called out all the children run around in the beginners' pool as fast as possible, making fighter jet noises and holding their arms stretched out backwards like a fighter plane's wings. As a contrast alternative, when the word "Sailplane" is called out, they all move around quietly and slowly. The arms are held out to the sides.

Fire-Water-Air
All the children run, hop or jump around in the beginners' pool. When the words "Fire", "Water" or "Air" are called out the following actions have to be taken: "Fire" - all run into a corner; "Water" - all run to the pool steps; "Air" - all lie down flat in the water.

Chain catch
A catcher starts catching people. Anyone caught has to hold on to the rear of the catcher so that, by and by, a long chain is formed. Only the free hands at the front of the chain may do the catching.
Variations:
- When the chain has reached 10 persons it can divide into two.
- Two catchers catch their own members for the chain. Which one can catch the most people and make the longest chain?

Strengthening games and games of motor skills
Pulling games
Two players face each other and hold their right hands. Each of them now tries to pull the other to his side.
Variations:
- Pull with the left hands.
- Do the exercise in pairs.

Topple your partner over
Two people face each other about 1m apart. They hold hands at about shoulder height. They now try to push each other so that one gets off balance and topples over.

Group pulling game
Two groups face each other across a gap. Each of them takes hold of the person standing in front of him to the right with his right hand and with his left hand he takes hold of the left hand of the person standing to the left front - a little like a zipper. Which group can pull the other over a predetermined line?

Group pushing game
Two groups face each other across a gap. Each of them takes hold of the person standing in front of him to the right with his right hand and with his left hand he takes hold of the left hand of the person standing to the left front - a little like a zipper, to be able to push the person on the opposite side with the hands. Which group can push the other over a predetermined line?

Further strengthening games and games of motor skills: Water polo, underwater polo - see RHEKER 2005 pp 115 et seq.

2. Long-term organic loading
When loading the body organically over the long-term, the cardiovascular system is stimulated in that one is on the move repeatedly for longer periods using the same rhythm. This can be done with alternating or static intensity.

Exercise examples
Swimming longer distances at a static or alternating intensity.
Training methods using stamina training, extensive interval training, sprints etc.
Game forms for swimming training - see Chapter 2.7.

3. Short-term, high-intensity demands on the muscles in the form of contracting and stretching exercises.
This form of relaxation is mainly carried out on dry land in the form of yoga - progressive muscle relaxation.

Further forms of relaxation include "passive, auto-suggestive, relaxation exercises" such as hypnosis, meditation, mental training and autogenic training (stereotyped exercises) (see HOFMANN 1977).

Practical examples of relaxation in water

Relaxation exercises in water can relieve tenseness and contribute towards a general feeling of well being, especially after the exertions of swimming training or intensive water gymnastics. Therefore, here are a few examples of relaxation exercises.

General conditions

Reasonable water temperature.
Sufficient room for movements.
No side noises (perhaps switch off the overflow to stop the noise).
Pleasant atmosphere using quiet music.

Personal situation

Being in the mood, prepared to relax.
Don't cramp up.
Remain calm, only do calm movements.

Picture 15: *Relaxing with a swimming noodle*

Exercise examples
Passive exercises in groups of three
The person in the middle lies stretched out between two helpers, who are holding him by the head and the feet and moving him gently (rocking motion).

Leading the blind
A helper pushes or pulls his partner through the water lying either on his stomach, his back or on his side and whose eyes are blindfolded or who is keeping his eyes shut.
Variations:
• The partner being pulled is lying on an airbed or a swimming board.
• The partner being pulled is wearing an aqua jogging belt.
• Two people pull another person who is lying in a relaxed position.

Relaxation and flotation aids
Using wobbly mats, swimming noodles or swimming boards relaxing positions are adopted in either a sitting or a lying down mode. A helper can move his partner through the water slowly.

Positions possible	
With a swmming noodle	Under the shoulders Under the neck
With two swimming noodles	Under the neck and the knee Under the shoulder and the bottom lenghtwise down the body
Three swimming noodles	Under the shoulder, the bottom and the feet.

The Impulses for Creative and Playful Swimming Training

2.7

"Many little steps let us move forward better than one large one."

Peter FRIEBE

Introduction

2.7.1

Swimming training doesn't need to be boring by sticking to monotonous training methods. Besides a variety of different swimming training methods there are numerous games and game forms that can brighten up the instruction.

Simultaneously, the playful approach to the medium of water will also bring some new experiences.

Playing in water opens up a whole variety of alternative approaches to the environment of water rather than the monotonous business of learning techniques and training with them. Learning by using a system oriented towards experiencing movement, one can realize many different other intensive feelings of moving in water and playing.

In the playful methods, the fun of moving and doing things together is at the forefront. Subsequently, the motivation of those being trained is enormously increased.

Also the area of swimming training can be linked together with the following pedagogic aspects to achieve different purposes:

Experiencing one's capability, understanding it and being able to judge it
Swimming training is particularly suitable for one to be able to experience one's own performance, understand it and be able to judge it. It can be improved by intensive forms of exercises.

Trying out things on one's own and being responsible
Swimming training assists one in establishing one's own limits and improves one's self-judgement. By training in a group one learns to become responsible for oneself and others.

Improving one's perception, broadening one's experience of moving
When swimming and training one learns new movement sequences. The perception of one's own body and the different possibilities that there are in moving in water can all be learned and broadened.

Cooperating, being competitive and communicating
This aspect is particularly true in training and competitive situations.

Supporting one's health, developing a health consciousness
A balanced program of swimming training supports good health for every age group from children up through to older people. It also develops a good degree of health consciousness in them.

2.7.2 The Forms of Movement for Swimming and Training

Playful forms of training and movement exercises encourage people to want to help in constructing the training sessions with their own ideas. These ideas for varying the training can be collected together and used in the program.

One can make a basic situation in swimming to be a problem and give the task to find a solution to this. The various solutions that people come up with can then be used as the basis for new game and exercise forms.

Making swimming easier
What can be done to make swimming easier?
    The participants of a training group can find out in a playful manner, what they have to do to make swimming easier. Equipment can be used that helps flotation.
Variations:
- Swim wearing different bathing wear.
- Swim in a neoprene swimsuit.
- Swimming with swimming boards under the stomach.
- Swimming with the aqua jogging belt.
- Swim a distance in the shortest time possible.
- Swim a distance in a time chosen by the swimmer.

- Swim a distance wearing flippers.
- Swim a distance underwater.
- Swimming using different positions: On the stomach, on the back, on the side, diagonally etc.
- Swimming a distance with a partner.
- Pulling the partner through the water e.g., with a rope.
- Swimming in saltwater.

Making swimming hard
What equipment can be used to make the water resistance higher so that it is harder to swim?

The participants of a training group can try to find out how to make swimming harder or how to increase the water resistance while swimming. Equipment can be used which hamper moving forwards and make swimming more difficult.

Variations:
- Swim wearing different bathing wear.
- Swim in life saving kit or a neoprene swimsuit.
- Swimming with flippers (and the mono flipper).
- Swimming with paddles.
- Swimming with weights.
- Swimming with a parachute.
- Swim, using only the arm movements and with a higher water resistance.
- Swim with the swimming board held sideways against the water.
- Swimming using different positions: On the stomach, on the back, on the side, diagonally etc.
- Swimming a distance together with a partner.

Swimming together or on one's own
Swim in pairs or in little groups trying out different ways of swimming forwards.
See later: "Games with a partner", "Group games".

Swimming a lane using the least number of strokes
Who can swim a set distance with the least number of strokes?
Variations:
- Swim using only the leg kick.

- Swim using only the arm strokes.
- Doing a swimming technique - arm and leg together.
- Doing different swimming strokes.

2.7.3 Game Forms for the Leg Kick

Relay races
Leg kick relay race
Several teams are formed that swim against each other in a relay race. A swimming board is used as a baton. First of all they swim using the leg strokes from the crawl.
Variations:
- Use different leg strokes: Crawl, backstroke, breaststroke or butterfly.
- Swim different distances: One, two or three widths.
- Swimming lengths, swimming with flippers (see Chapter 2.1.8).

Holding the swimming board sideways
Several teams are formed that swim against each other in a relay race. A swimming board is used as a baton, held in such a position that it is sideways to the direction being swum.
Variations:
- Use different leg strokes: Crawl, backstroke, breaststroke or butterfly.
- Swim different distances: see above.
- Hold the swimming board in different ways:
- Vertically in the water.
- Diagonally in the water.

Carrying relay race
Objects are used as a baton in a relay race (pull buoy, swimming board, ball).
Variations:
- Swim a width.
- Swim a length.
- Carrying several objects at the same time.

Obstacle relay race
Several teams are formed that swim against each other in an obstacle relay race. A pull buoy or a swimming board etc., is used as a baton.
Variations: See above.

Swimming vertically
All the swimmers try to raise themselves up out of the water by just using the crawl leg kick.
Variations:
- Swimming vertically using the butterfly kick.
- Swimming vertically using the breaststroke kick.
- Swimming vertically treading water.
- Keeping the arms in the water when swimming vertically.
- Holding one arm high up out of the water when swimming vertically.
- Both arms are held up high.
- Who can get the furthest out of the water?
- Who can hold his arms up the longest and keep the head (upper body) above the water?

Diving underwater: A relay race underwater using the leg kick: Using flippers, doing a slalom, diving with a partner etc - see Chapter 2.1.8.

Games with the swimming board
Jousting knights
Each swimmer sits on a swimming board and tries to move himself through the water. Who can knock the other swimmers off their swimming board?
Variations:
- Jousting Knights as a team game: One team rides on blue swimming boards, the other on red ones. Which team manages to keep most of their 'Knights' mounted on the boards in a laid down time?
- Jousting Knights competition: Each team sends only one of their 'Knights' forward at any time to joust with a swimmer from the other team.

Games with a partner
Pushing game using the leg kick
Two swimmers take hold of opposite sides of a swimming board and each tries to push the other away. They begin the game in the middle of the pool. Who can push his partner to the side of the pool first?
Variations:
• Pushing the partner away using the breaststroke leg kick.
• Pushing the partner away using the butterfly leg kick.
• Pushing the partner away using the backstroke leg kick.
• Pushing the partner away up to a particular mark.
• Two swimmers take hold of each other by the upper arms and try to push the partner away using leg kicks.

Who is the strongest leg kick swimmer?
Play the 'pushing game using the leg kick' as above. Several pairs are doing the exercise on the center line of the pool. After about 2 minutes the winner will have been found. The winner changes over with the next man in the lineup, moving his position towards the starting blocks. The loser drops one place in the opposite direction and also is now facing a new opponent. After several run-throughs both the strongest leg kickers will be facing each other and the overall winner will be found.

Pushing the partner
A swimmer tries to push his partner through the water.
Variations:
• Pushing the partner using the breaststroke leg kick.
• Pushing the partner using the crawl leg kick.
• Pushing the partner using the butterfly leg kick.
• Pushing the partner using the backstroke leg kick.
• Pushing the partner using the crawl leg kick wearing flippers.

Group games
Pushing the other group away using the leg kick
Two groups face each other across a gap. Each swimmer takes hold of the person's hand opposite him to the right with his right hand and with his left hand he takes hold of the left hand of the person to his left like a zipper. The hands are bent so that they press against each other.

Which group can push the other back to the side of the pool using the crawl leg kick?
Variations:
- All use the breaststroke leg kick.
- All use the butterfly leg kick.
- All the swimmers hold on to a swimming board.
- All swim using flippers or the mono-flipper.

Lifting the circle
6-8 people form a circle. The swimmers are holding hands and attempt, using the crawl leg kick to lift themselves up out of the water.
Variations:
- Which circle of swimmers can get the highest up out of the water?
- Which circle stays up in the air the longest?
- Swim vertically using the butterfly leg kick.
- Swim vertically using the breaststroke leg kick.
- All the swimmers in the circle hold their arms up high.

Mexican wave using the leg kick
6-8 people form a circle. All swim in the vertical position and one after the other lift oneself high up out of the water using the crawl leg kick - just like in the Mexican wave.
Variations:
- Which circle of people can keep the Mexican wave going for the longest?
- Which circle of people can get up the highest out of the water when doing the wave?
- After lifting themselves up each swimmer submerges himself.
- Doing the Mexican wave with the butterfly leg kick.
- Doing the Mexican wave with the breaststroke leg kick.

Game Forms for the Arm Stroke   2.7.4

Relay races
Arm stroke relay race
Several teams are formed that swim against each other in relay races. A pull buoy is used as a baton. First of all all of them swim using the arm stroke from the crawl.

Variations:
- Use different arm stroke styles: Crawl, backstroke, breaststroke or butterfly.
- Different distances are swum: One, two or three widths.
- Swim lengths.

Arm stroke obstacle race

Several teams are formed that swim against each other in an obstacle race. Obstacles are slalom poles, mats/airbeds (which have to be swum underneath), tires (which to be swum through) etc. First of all all of them swim using the arm stroke from the crawl.
Variations: see above.

Throwing the dice

Each team has a dice. The first person in the team throws the dice and then has to swim the same number of lengths shown by the dice. The team that wins is the one in which all the members manage to swim the number of lengths corresponding to the dice.
Variations: see above.

Diving underwater

Underwater diving relay race
Several teams are formed and they do an underwater diving relay race. First of all they do the breaststroke arm movements.
Variations:
- Use different arm strokes: Breaststroke or dog paddle.
- Use the arm stroke and the leg kick.
- Do the game over different distances: One, two or three widths.
- Dive underwater down a length.
- Dive underwater round a slalom course.

Games with a partner

Pulling game using only the arm stroke
Two swimmers hook their feet together and try, using the crawl arm stroke, to pull their partner away. They begin from the center of the swimming pool. Who can pull his partner first to the side of the pool?
Variations:
- Pulling the partner with the breaststroke arm movements.

- Pulling the partner with the butterfly arm stroke.
- Pulling the partner with the backstroke arm movements.
- Pulling the partner over a specific mark.

Towing the partner
A swimmer tries to tow his partner through the water, who is holding on to him by the leg.
Variations:
- Pulling the partner with the breaststroke arm movements.
- Pulling the partner with the crawl arm stroke.
- Pulling the partner with the butterfly arm stroke.
- Pulling the partner with the backstroke arm movements.
- Pulling the partner over one or more lengths.

Swimming with the partner in the same rhythm
A pair tries to swim a particular distance using the same swimming technique and stays in rhythm with each other.
Variations:
- Swimming with the partner using the breaststroke.
- Swimming with the partner using the crawl.
- Swimming with the partner using the water polo crawl stroke.
- Swimming with the partner using the butterfly stroke.
- Swimming with the partner using the backstroke.
- Swimming with the partner using different strokes.
- Swimming with the partner on different paths (straight, in a slalom etc.).
- Swimming with the partner at different speeds.

Group games - see Chapter 2.7.6.

Game Forms for Coordination

2.7.5

Relay races
A relay race to train the coordination
Several teams are formed which race against each other in a relay race. All swim using the crawl.
Variations:
- All swim the breaststroke.

- All swim the crawl.
- All swim the butterfly.
- All swim the backstroke.
- All swim different strokes.
- Each person in the group swims a different stroke. When there are more than 4 persons swimming, different techniques can be combined e.g., the arm stroke from the crawl with the leg actions of the butterfly.
- Swimming with the partner on different paths (straight, in a slalom etc.).

Medley relay 1
Four swimmers of a team swim using different strokes. Different distances are covered; one, two or three widths/lengths.

Medley relay 2
Several teams of each four swimmers do a relay race against each other.
   The first swimmer does the back crawl, the second the breaststroke, the third the butterfly and the fourth the crawl.
Variations:
- All swim and change their techniques as they do.
- At the start of each person the technique he is to use is set.
- Swimming with the partner on different paths (straight, in a slalom etc.).
- Do the race over different distances: One, two or three widths.
- Swim lengths.
- Obstacles have to be swum round.

Tucking in behind
The swimmers in a team have, like in all relay races, to swim a particular distance in the shortest time possible. In the 'tucking in behind' relay race game, the first swimmer swims round a marker and goes back to collect the next swimmer. Both swim off again round the marker together and fetch the third swimmer and so on until all have been collected etc.
Variations:
- When all the players have been collected i.e., 'tucked in behind', they are then 'dropped off' in the reverse order.
- The swimmers can use different techniques of swimming.

Games with equipment

Swimming board relay race
A swimming board is used as a baton in a relay race.
Variations:
- Swim a width.
- Swim a length.
- Pass on different objects (swimming board, pull buoy, ball).
- Swimming using different styles: Crawl, back crawl, butterfly or breaststroke.
- Carrying more than one object at the same time.
- In all, five objects have to be moved. The first swimmer collects one particular object, the second swimmer a different one and so on. The following objects can be carried by each team: Swimming board, pull buoy, ball, diving ring, flippers.
- Swim round obstacles.

Relay racing in clothes
In this relay race, the first swimmer from each team wears a T-shirt, a bathing cap and flippers. He then swims to a marker, round it and back again, where he passes the clothes on to the next person. The winning team is the one that gets its clothed swimmers through first.
Variations:
- Wear life saving clothes and equipment (jacket, pants) including flippers.
- You can use funny seasonal clothing e.g., carnival costume, Christmas themes etc.

Moving pull buoys
The children use a pull buoy in a relay race.
Variations:
- The pull buoys are carried so that they do not get wet.
- The pull buoys are moved along underwater.
- Different distances are swum: One, two or three widths or lengths.
- Using different swimming styles: Crawl, back crawl, breaststroke or the butterfly.

Egg and spoon race

Each child has a spoon, on which they balance a tennis ball. Who can swim a width without losing the ball off the spoon?

Variations:
- Swim a length.
- Do it as a relay race.
- Swim round obstacles.

Carrying objects

A diving ring is balanced on top of the head and carried backwards and forwards like this. The hands may not touch or hold on to the ring.

Balloon relay race

A balloon, filled with gas and tied to a string, is used as the baton in a relay race.

Carrying a matchbox

A box of matches is used as a baton in a relay race. When all the swimmers are done swimming, a candle is lit on the edge of the pool.

The candle relay

A lit candle is used as a baton in a relay race. If the candle goes out while a swimmer is doing his turn, he has to swim back to the edge of the pool and lighten it up again.

Variations:
- A burning tea-light candle is moved as the baton on a swimming board.
- The first swimmer has to carry one tea-light, the second swimmer two candles etc., until the fourth swimmer can light the final large candle.

Passing the ball on

Teams are formed, with one half of each team split on each opposite side of the pool. The first swimmer, pushing a ball in the water, from one side starts off and meets his counterpart from the other side halfway across. He takes on the ball and swims back to his side. As soon as he touches the side with his hand the next team member can swim off.

Variation:
- Use different swimming styles: Water polo stroke, water polo dribbling style or pushing the ball along using the sidestroke.

Games for Training

Games for individual training
Reduced arm strokes
Each swimmer swims a lane using the crawl and counts the number of arm strokes he takes to do this. The next time he does this, he has to swim the same distance using one arm stroke less.

Variations:
- Who can swim the lane with one or two arm strokes of the crawl less?
- Do it with the breaststroke.
- Do it with underwater arm strokes.
- Do it with the butterfly stroke.
- Do it with the crawl arm stroke and the butterfly leg kick.
- Do it with the crawl arm stroke and the breaststroke leg kick.
- Do it with the breaststroke arm stroke and the crawl leg kick.
- Other combinations.

One leg kick less
Each swimmer swims a lane using the breaststroke and counts the number of leg kicks he needs to do. The next time he does this, he has to swim the same distance one leg kick less.
Variations: See above.

The breathing pyramid
One of the swimmers begins by doing two strokes for each breath he takes. Then he increases this to three strokes, four strokes up to six strokes or eight strokes. He then reduces little by little back to two strokes.
Variation:
- Each lane he does two strokes per breath then three strokes, up to ten strokes.

Swimming the screw thread

A swimmer swims so that for every arm stroke he takes he turns his body over half a turn from lying on the stomach to turning onto the back and then over again back onto the stomach.

Variations:

- Swim a predetermined number of 'screw turns' down a lane of the pool e.g., 4 screw turns.
- Do two screw turns to the left and two screw turns to the right down a lane.
- Other combinations.

Pyramid swimming

The swimmers swim distances which are progressively longer and then shorter e.g., 25m, 50m, 75m, 100m, 75m, 50m, 25m.

Variations:

- The gaps in the distance remain the same.
- The speed is always the same.
- The gaps and speed can be varied.
- The distances can be increased 50m, 100m, 150m, 200m, 250m, 200m, 150m, 100m, 50m.

Interval swimming

In "interval swimming", the swimmer changes his speeds. He is swimming a longer distance e.g., 3000m and swims intervals at different speeds, sometimes faster sometimes slower. The intervals can be changed at will.

Variations:

- Swim two lanes slowly and then one lane fast (20 x).
- Swim four lanes slowly, two lanes fast (10 x).
- Increase the speed just before each turn at the end of the lane and then slow down again after the turn.
- Swim regular and irregular intervals as one pleases.

Games with a partner

Swimming in pairs

A partner holds on to the legs of the swimmer in front of him. The front man does the arm strokes from the breaststroke technique while the man behind does the leg kicks.

Variations:
- The swimming styles can be varied: Breaststroke, crawl, butterfly, backstroke crawl.
- The techniques can be mixed: Arm stroke from the crawl with butterfly leg kicks, breaststroke arm strokes with crawl leg kicks.

Synchronized swimming with a partner
Two swimmers swim alongside each other and try to synchronize all their movements together.

Catch up swimming
One swimmer starts off two meters behind his partner and tries to catch up with him. When he reaches him he grabs hold of his legs and pulls himself forwards. Then he will have the lead and the partner now has to try to catch up with him.

Catch up swimming and diving
Two swimmers sprint after each other. When the one behind catches up with the front man and touches him he then dives forward underwater. The rear man now has the lead and the one who he dived under has to now repeat the process to catch up.

Couple coordination
Two swimmers are holding onto a swimming board and swim alongside each other. The swimmer on the left holds onto the swimming board with his right hand and the swimmer on the right-hand side holds onto it with his left hand. Each of their free arms does the crawl stroke and they also do the leg kick.
Variations:
- Crawl arm stroke with the butterfly leg kick.
- Crawl arm stroke with the breaststroke leg kick.
- Breaststroke arm stroke with the breaststroke leg kick.
- Breaststroke arm stroke with the butterfly leg kick.
- Breaststroke arm stroke with the crawl leg kick.
- Other combinations.

Fewer arm strokes
One of the partners tries to swim a lane (25m) with the least number of arm strokes. The other partner counts the number of arm strokes.

Variations:

- Crawl arm strokes.
- Breaststroke arm strokes.
- Swimming under water with arm strokes.
- Butterfly arm strokes.
- Crawl arm stroke with the butterfly leg kick.
- Crawl arm stroke with the breaststroke leg kick.
- Breaststroke arm stroke with the breaststroke leg kick.
- Breaststroke arm stroke with the butterfly leg kick.
- Breaststroke arm stroke with the crawl leg kick.
- Other combinations.

Group games

Meeting in the middle

Several teams are formed. Each team divides into half, with each half standing on the opposite edge of the pool. The game starts with two swimmers, one from each half of each team, swimming towards each other to meet in the centre of the lane. After meeting in the centre both swimmers swim back to their sides. As the swimmer reaches his side of the pool the next one starts. The winning team is the one in which the last two swimmers meet in the middle first.

Variations:

- The swimming styles can be varied: Breaststroke, crawl, butterfly, backstroke crawl.
- Swimming using only arm strokes.
- Swimming using only leg kicks.
- Swimming with flippers.
- Swimming with paddles.
- Swimming in clothes.

Slalom sprinting

5-9 swimmers swim along loosely behind each other at a reasonable speed. The last swimmer now tries to swim forward, sprinting to overtake the others in a slalom motion. When the swimmer gets to the front the next one starts.

Variations: See above.

Last man forward

A group of 4-6 swimmers swim along behind each other at a medium speed. The last one in the group now sprints past the others to the front. When he gets to the front then the last man does the same.
Variations: See above.

Numbers race

2-4 teams each form a circle. Each member of each team is given a number. When the instructor calls out a number, that person has to swim once round the circle and back to his place.
Variations:
- The teams line up by the starting blocks. The person whose number is called out has to swim a lane.
- The swimmers have to do more than one length.
- The distances have to be swum using different swimming styles.

Further games: "Gap in the circle", "Medley relay", "Number race with flippers", "Water polo relay", "Water biathlon", "Water polo".

Games with equipment
Resistance swimming

A rubber bungee rope is tied to the swimmer's ankle. He now tries to swim as far away as possible against the resistance of the bungee and maintains this position against the resistance by keeping swimming.

Jute bag swimming

A swimmer puts his feet through the handles of a jute bag and tries to swim the crawl down one or more lanes against the resistance that is built up by the bag.
Variations:
- The swimming styles can be varied: Breaststroke, crawl, butterfly.
- Swimming using the back crawl.
- Swimming with paddles.
- Swimming wearing more clothes.
- Swimming using only a leg kick while holding the jute bag stretched out in front.
- Varying the swimming style.

- Swimming with flippers.
- Doing a relay race with either only arm strokes or leg kicks.

Passing the weight
A group of swimmers form a circle in the pool. Holding up their arms they all try to keep their arms above the water by kicking and treading the water. A weight e.g., a water polo ball is passed round the circle and each swimmer has to hold it up in the air for 5 seconds. All the others count the seconds down out loud.
Variations:
- The swimming styles can be varied: Breaststroke leg kick, crawl, butterfly leg kick, treading water etc.
- An underwater polo ball is passed round.
- A diving ring (5 kg) is passed round.

'Making swimming easier' and Making swimming harder' see Chapter 2.7.2.

2.7.7   'Little' & 'Big' Games for Water Sports to Improve Fitness

Many games can be used, which can be found in the large palette of games in water with a ball. These give more fun when swimming and training or give fresh motivation for the coming season. Above all, when doing swimming training they are very useful to complement the other exercises.

Because these games were covered in Volume 2 (RHEKER 2005), at this juncture we only draw attention to them.

'Little' games with a ball
➤ Throwing at a target (RHEKER 2005, pp 112-115).
➤ 'Tiger ball' games (RHEKER 2005, p 118).
➤ Passing the ball (RHEKER 2005, pp 118-120).
➤ Water basketball (RHEKER 2005, pp 128-129).
➤ Water polo (RHEKER 2005, pp 117 et seq).
➤ Water biathlon (RHEKER 2005, p 131).
➤ Underwater polo (RHEKER 2005, p 174).

3 The Playful Way of Learning to do the Butterfly Stroke

"Water can exist without fish,
but fish cannot exist without water"

Chinese proverb

Preliminary remarks
The butterfly stroke is a style on its own where the whole body is involved in the stroke. The movements in the stroke are not made up of the individual motions of the leg kick or the arm stroke. In order to be able to swim the butterfly well, the requirement is for a strong wriggling motion performed by the whole body.

This is why it is necessary to come up with a suitable method of learning the stroke. This is unlike the other styles, where the various elements of the strokes can be learned initially in isolation (e.g., leg kick and arm stroke) leading up to practicing the complete coordination of the stroke with the correct breathing method. Rather, a unique method is required to bring the swimmer on with the butterfly stroke.

The following methods are the best used:
➤ Methodical lead to the butterfly stroke via the dolphin dive.
➤ Methodical lead to the butterfly stroke with the aid of flippers.
➤ A learning program for the butterfly stroke.
➤ Methodical lead up the butterfly stroke via the breaststroke.

In particular, the methods using the dolphin dive and the flipper method offer many opportunities to learn the butterfly stroke in a playful manner.

Therefore, these methods are explained in full. The basis for the instruction is by way of a series of methodical exercises where, in this book, the playful element is concentrated upon.

A Methodical Way of Approaching the Butterfly Stroke via the Dolphin Dive

3.1

At the beginning of the explanations on the methodical approach to learning the butterfly stroke are the games and game forms. By correctly doing the dolphin dive, the basic motion of the body with the wriggling movement is practiced. The posture of the head is very important in this. The exercise "Doing the dolphin dive down to the bottom of the pool" leads up to the initial coordination of the leg kick movement and the pressure phase of the arm stroke, which is achievable in this method without practically any problem. Exercise 10 (The dolphin dive and the following double leg kick) and Exercise 11 (The dolphin dive and the double leg kick) are of particular importance for learning the double-tact rhythm (two leg kicks to each thrust of the arms) and must be intensively practiced. After the rhythm has been learned by the simple method of using the dolphin dive, the remainder of the motion of the arms can be added. At the end of the learning process, the rhythmical breathing system has to be learned and coordinated with the whole stroke.

By constant repetition over short distances, with eventual corrections being applied, the butterfly stroke can be improved upon. By increasing the distances to be covered doing the stroke, this will firm up the perfection of the style. At the end of the chapter, there are suggestions of some games and game forms that will improve stamina while doing this stroke.

Playful Forms of the Dolphin Dive

3.1.1

The following games using the dolphin dive are suitable as a basis, in playful form, for leading up to learning the butterfly stroke.

Diving like dolphins

All the children dive like dolphins in the beginners' pool. Using the freely constructed exercises, the children can try out copying how they think dolphins dive in the water. The exact movements are covered in Chapter 3.1.2.

Variations:
- Diving like a dolphin in different directions.
- Diving in like a dolphin making the least amount of splash.
- Doing dolphin dives through hoops.
- Doing several dolphin dives one after the other through several hoops.
- Doing a dolphin dive in different ways: Forwards, sideways, backwards or by doing a twisting movement along the axis of the body. (Take care not to collide with others!)

Holes in the ice
Several tires are floating on the surface of the water and these represent holes in the ice. The children have to dive underwater and surface up through the 'ice holes'. As they emerge up through the inner tube they do a dive like a dolphin.

The dolphin dive
Two children are holding a pole, rope or hoop between them. A third child dives in like a dolphin from the pool steps through the hoop (or over the rope/pole) into the water.
Variations:
- Doing a dolphin dive through a hoop.
- Doing several dolphin dives one after the other through several hoops.
- Doing a dolphin dive in different ways: Forwards, sideways, backwards or by doing a twisting movement along the axis of the body.

Diving through the partner's split legs
A person is standing with his legs wide apart in the splits so that his partner can dive through his legs.
Variations:
- Dive over a pole being held by the partner and then dive down through the legs of another person.
- Doing a dolphin dive through a hoop and then dive down through the partner's legs.

Catching and diving underwater
A catcher tries to catch as many swimmers as he can. Those who have their head under the water cannot be caught.

Variations:
Those standing on their hands in the water cannot be caught.
Those sitting on the bottom cannot be caught.

Catching dolphins
All the children dive in the beginners' pool like dolphins. A child is nominated as the catcher and is distinguished by wearing a colored swimming cap. As soon as the catcher catches a 'dolphin', the person he catches becomes the new catcher.
Variations:
- Anyone caught becomes a catcher together with the others caught before.
- You are only allowed to tab the other players by touching them above the belt line.
- Those standing on their hands in the water cannot be caught.
- Those sitting on the bottom cannot be caught.
- The number of catchers can be increased.

Figures of eight
A swimmer dives underwater and does a figure of the number eight through the legs of his partner.
Variations:
- Doing the figure of the number eight with the sidestroke.
- Doing the figure of the number eight with the backstroke.
- Doing the figure of the number eight wearing flippers.

The eel
A child wriggles like an eel between members of the group standing around in the water.

Underwater pothole swimming
Two or three children stand behind each other and each of them is holding a hoop. The other children now try to dive underwater through these hoops.
Variations:
- Five hoops are held in the water.
- You can only surface through one of the hoops that is lying on the water.
- Hoops held vertically and horizontally have to be dived through.
- The 'pothole' has curves in it.
- There is a 'treasure' sitting at the end of the pothole, which has to be brought to the surface.

3.1.2   Methodical Exercises and Games for the Butterfly

After having gained various experiences by playing using the dolphin dive, we learn the butterfly stroke by means of simple forms of the dolphin dive in the following section. The simple movements of the dolphin dive are worked on and lead up to the butterfly stroke by using the main characteristics of the movements. They start with simple steps, moving on to more complex ones and end up by coordinating the whole stroke.

Exercise 1: Doing dolphin dives making as little a splash as possible
The children dive like dolphins so they make as little splash as possible. Take-off is done by pushing up with both legs from the bottom of the beginners' pool.

In this way the criteria for good dolphin dives can be practiced together with the possibility of carrying out additional movements and corrections:

Watch out in which position your head is in when you do a successful dive without splashing (the head should be between the arms and chin on the chest).

How did your body enter the water? The body should follow the line of the hands as it enters the water.

How is the body held as it dives down into the water? Body tensed in a bow and stomach pulled in with the back rounded.

Variations:
- Doing dolphin dives in different directions.
- Doing dolphin dives through hoops.
- Doing several dolphin dives, one after the other, through several hoops.
- Doing dolphin dives in different ways: Forwards, sideways, backwards or with a twist of the body along the axis of the body. (Take care to avoid a collision with others!)

Exercise 2: Doing dolphin dives as above, swinging the arms forward flat as you take off
Do Exercise 1 above and its variations. However, this time make sure that as you take off to do the dive, the arms are brought from the sides and swung forward flat while the chin is placed on the chest.

By doing this you bring your body into the correct tensed position. At the same time you learn to coordinate the swing of the arms, the position of the head and the chin on the chest.

Exercise 3: Doing dolphin dives with outside assistance
This time you do dolphin dives through tires that are lying on the water. A child, acting as an assistant, holds two tubes about 1m apart. The other child dives in through the first tube and resurfaces up through the second one. As he dives in, the chin is held on the chest and as he resurfaces in the second tube the head is tilted back into the nape of the neck.

Exercise 4: Diving down to the bottom of the pool with a dolphin dive
After mastering the dolphin dive in its basic form, you are now ready to move on to the next step. In this method, the next step is to coordinate the leg kick movement and the pull of the arms.

Do dolphin dives as in Exercises 2 & 3 above ending up each time on the bottom of the pool. Now push off sharply with both hands from the bottom of the pool. As you do this, the head is taken back into the nape of the neck. As soon as sufficient accent has been placed on getting the position of the head right (chin on chest when diving in, head into the nape of the neck when pushing off with the hands), then we can begin with the coordination of the arms and legs i.e., the leg is practically automatically done as the arms pull back.

Exercise 5: Consciously coordinating the leg kick with the pull of the arms
Coordination of the leg kick and the arm pull that was mechanically taking place in the previous exercise is now carried out consciously in this phase. A well-performed demonstration of the movement will help to make it clear to the pupil.

When it becomes clear from practicing the movement that adequate control of the head automatically leads on to the coordination of the pulling phase with the arms and the leg kick, then all the children can concentrate on consciously continuing to practice this movement.

Exercise 6: Further practice of coordinating the leg kick with the pull of the arms

After having achieved a good coordination of the dolphin leg kick with the pull of the arms in the previous exercise, this can now be concentrated on by practicing it further. For this the children can be instructed to accentuate the leg kick during the arm pull phase.

Exercise 7: Doing a flat dolphin dive

The dolphin dives that were carried out in Exercises 4-6 are now executed flatter in this exercise. The pupil no longer dives down to the bottom of the pool. As soon as the body is immersed after the dive, the arm pull takes place while the head is brought back into the nape of the neck. In this way, the leg kick automatically comes in with the arm pull phase.

Exercise 8: Practicing the arm pull

No one should have a wrong imagination of the arm pull so the optimum pattern of it is practiced at this point. Therefore, it should be demonstrated by one of the pupils who has proved a good pattern of the movement. Following this demonstration (or any other form of showing the movement), the others begin to learn the movement themselves in simple situations:

The arm pull is broken down into simple, controlled movements – legs bent and the upper body lying on the surface of the water. For this, different points can be followed:

1. The arm pull phase: After the hands and the arms enter the water in front of the shoulders, the hands are turned a little outwards and begin to pull back in a gentle arc. By increasing the bend of the hands they are pulled slightly inwards and the arms form a right angle about the height of the shoulders. Now the transition is made to exerting pressure in the arm-pulling phase.

2. The pressure phase: Following the arm-pulling phase, the arms are stretched and pulled downwards and backwards until they reach the thighs. The arm pull phase and the pressure phase are shaped like a key hole pattern.

3. The swing forward phase: After the pressure phase, the hands are brought forward from the hips in a swinging movement.

Exercise 9: Doing a dolphin dive with accent on the arm pull phase
The flat dolphin dive carried out in Exercise 7 is now coordinated with the complete arm pull phase.

Exercise 10: Doing a dolphin dive and going on to do a second leg kick
This step in the method is a very important one for learning the double kick rhythm. The dolphin dive is carried out as practiced in the previous exercise. After the pressure phase, where the head is brought back into the nape of the neck, the head is lifted up as the arms stretch and then the forehead is placed down in the water again. The chin is brought down onto the chest. The hands remain on the thighs. As the forehead comes down into the water a new wave of the movement is started ending with a second kick of the legs. When the wave-like movement of the whole body is discernible, then one can start practicing the next step.

Exercise 11: Doing the dolphin dive and the second leg kick
The dolphin dive is done as in the previous exercise, however this time when the head is immersed, the arms are swung forward and stay there until the second leg kick is discernible by the wave-like movement caused by bringing down the chin onto the chest.

Exercise 12: Doing the dolphin dive and the second pull of the arms
When the second leg kick, done as the hands enter the water, has been learned then the second arm stroke can be added. Now it is possible to do two dolphin like movements one after the other in a double-tact rhythm.

Exercise 13: Doing the dolphin dive and several arm strokes
When the double-tact rhythm, as described in the previous exercise, can be done successfully, then this can be combined with several arm strokes.

Exercise 14: Learning the correct breathing
Playful forms for learning to breathe correctly in water were covered in Volume 1 (RHEKER "First Steps" 2004). Here, it is a question of learning the correct method for the butterfly. The children should

have learned what method is used to teach this swimming technique; breathe out long into the water and then take a short breath in.

This rhythmical kind of breathing can be practiced again using the following games and exercise forms:

Exercise 15: Rhythmical breathing
The children have to carry out the exercise of breathing out for a long time in water and taking a short breath in:
- On the surface of the water, breathe out for a long time and then take a short breath in.
- Hold on to the edge of the pool and breathe out for a long time into the water, then lift the head up and take a short breath in.
- Holding yourself in a push-up position at the pool steps: Breathe out for a long time into the water and take a short breath in.
- Lie the head on the water as you walk along. Breathe out long into the water and then take a short breath in.
- One partner pulls the other by the stretched arms through the water. The one being pulled practices breathing out for a long time and then taking a short breath in.

As in all the exercises, it should be regular practice to learn to breathe out through the nose and the mouth, while breathing in is done through the mouth only. When doing these exercises, the breathing out phase should always be twice as long as the breathing in phase. So that the swimming style can be properly coordinated, it is important that the breathing rhythm for the particular swimming style is done correctly.

Further exercises and games to practice rhythmical breathing
Using a partner to help, squat down and breathe out.
Alternate diving and breathing.
Play the fireman's pump game.

Exercise 16: Coordination of the breathing rhythm needed to do the butterfly stroke
Now when you breathe, the head has to be moved as is required in the butterfly stroke. The rhythmical breathing done in the butterfly stroke is very similar to the breathing movement done in the

breaststroke. When breathing in the head is lifted up and when breathing out the head is laid into the water. This can all be practiced separately in the water.

Variations:

- Holding yourself in a push-up position face down at the pool steps: Breathe out for a long time into the water and then lift the head and take a short breath in.
- Break down the actions: Breathe out for a long time in the water and then lift the head up quickly to take a short breath in.
- One partner pulls the other by the stretched out arms through the water. The one being pulled practices breathing out for a long time and then takes a short breath in.
- As above, but now adding the leg kick.
- Breaking down the actions by now adding the arm stroke.

Exercise 17: Doing the butterfly now coordinated with breathing
Rhythmical breathing is now combined with doing the whole of the butterfly technique. First of all short distances are swum. As confidence grows, the distances can be increased.

Exercise 18: Regular repeats over short distances
So that the movement sequence of the butterfly technique is properly internalized and a good feeling for the technique is developed, after learning to do the butterfly stroke only short distances should be swum so that no mistakes begin to appear caused by exhaustion. By doing regular repeats of short stretches, and with the appropriate corrections being made, the style can be improved and learned well.

Exercise 19: Increasing the swum distance
After improvements and learning has been completed as in the previous exercise, the swum distance using this stroke can be increased gradually so that the style will become automatic.

Exercise 20: Improving stamina
See the playful methods of training exercises for improving stamina in Chapter 2.7.6.
- The breathing pyramid.

- Pyramid swimming.
- Interval swimming.
- Swimming in pairs.
- Swimming relay races etc.

Exercise 21: Variations of the butterfly stroke technique

The coordination ability of a swimmer can be improved by practicing various different techniques. The following suggestions for variations of the butterfly stroke are listed here:
- Variation of the technique: Doing short and long pulls of the arm.
- Swimming the butterfly stroke backwards.
- Doing the butterfly stroke using the arm movements of the crawl.
- Doing the butterfly arm stroke with the leg kick from the crawl.
- Doing the butterfly arm stroke with the leg kick from the breaststroke.
- Chasing dolphins: See earlier "Catching dolphins".

Exercise 22: Increasing performance using games and exercise forms

The following exercise and game forms contribute to improving the technique and at the same time they will heighten motivation by having fun doing them.

Relay races
Relay racing in clothes

In this relay race, the first swimmer in each team wears a T-shirt, a bathing cap and flippers. He then swims to a marker, round it and back again, where he passes the clothing on to the next person. The winning team is the one that gets its clothed swimmers through first.
Variations:
- Wear life saving clothes and equipment (jacket, pants) including flippers.
- You can use funny seasonal clothing e.g., carnival costume, Christmas themes etc.

Tucking in behind

The swimmers in a team have, like in all relay races, to swim a particular distance in the shortest time possible. In the 'tucking in behind' relay race game, the first swimmer swims round a marker and goes back to collect the next swimmer. Both swim off again round the marker together and fetch the third swimmer and so on until all have been collected etc.

Variations:

- When all the players have been collected i.e., 'tucked in behind', they are then 'dropped off' in the reverse order.
- The swimmers can use different techniques of swimming.

Further relay races: There are numerous relay races described throughout the book - almost all of them are very suitable for intensive training and can be adapted for this purpose very easily.

The Advantages and Disadvantages of the Butterfly Stroke   3.1.3

Table 2: *The advantages and disadvantages of the dolphin dive method*

Advantages	Disadvantages
• Using the dolphin dive method can already be integrated in the games and game forms met in beginners' swimming and provide a basic sounding for the butterfly stroke from the beginning. • The dolphin dive method comes over well with children because it integrates a lot of games. • The wave-like movement of the body can be clearly discerned. • The coordination of the leg kick and the pull of the arms in the pressure phase come together in this method practically automatically.	• The second leg kick (done as the hands enter the water) is not so easy to learn as it is by using the method where flippers are worn (flipper method). • The wave-like movement is very often made too long between the dolphin dive and the diving down to the bottom of the pool.

- The dolphin dive method is also very suitable for beginner swimmers. Because there are lots of games and exercises involved, also in the beginners' pool, learning the stroke is not so tiring as in other sterile exercise forms.
- By using the dolphin dive the child gets more forward drive than starting off lying on the surface.
- One starts to learn with exercises that are already well-known from beginners' instruction (first lessons in diving underwater, gliding in the water, diving down headfirst etc.).
- The dolphin dive method is a comprehensive method to learn the butterfly stroke.

3.2 The Methodical Way of Learning the Butterfly Using Flippers

The flipper method or the wriggling method is also a comprehensive method of learning to swim the butterfly stroke. The wriggling movement as a basis of the butterfly technique is first of all done with the help of flippers. This can be practiced in different swimming styles.

Because many children find it easier to do the wriggling movement in the backstroke or sidestroke mode, they should be allowed to try out any method while using the flippers.

After learning the rhythm of the leg kick movements, there are two ways to move on from there into the full coordination of the stroke:

๏ In combination with the double-tact rhythm, the crawl arm stroke is used.

๏ During the wriggling movement, the butterfly arm stroke is added.

After the breathing rhythm has been learned, then this is also added into the work on the coordination of the movement. Just as in the previous chapter with the dolphin dive method, games and exercise forms are used to work on the full coordination of the stroke.

Theoretical Introduction to Using Flippers

3.2.1

Before children swim for the first time with flippers, they must receive a little basic instruction on how to use them:

๏ You should never run on dry land with flippers on, because there is great danger of falling over wearing them.

๏ Running in flippers can damage them.

๏ The flippers should always be put on in a sitting position on the edge of the pool i.e., putting them on in the water.

๏ Using flippers to swim with makes you very fast, therefore, you must always watch where you are going and swim with care when wearing them.

๏ Swimming in flippers takes a lot of energy. This can lead easily to cramps in the legs for those who are not used to wear them.

Practical Exercises for Using Flippers

3.2.2

To get used to flippers, first of all the children can use the swimming strokes they already know. This can be done in the following games and exercise forms:

Swimming the crawl leg kick with flippers
First of all, swim a width on the stomach wearing flippers and doing the crawl leg kick.
Variations:
• Crawl leg kick wearing flippers on the back over a length.
• Crawl leg kick wearing flippers over several lengths.

- Crawl leg kick wearing flippers using the sidestroke over one or several lengths.
- Crawl leg kick wearing one flipper on the stomach over one or several lengths.
- Crawl leg kick underwater in different body positions.

Swimming the crawl leg kick with flippers as a relay race
- Doing the crawl leg kick lying on the stomach.
- Doing the crawl leg kick lying on the back.
- Doing the crawl leg kick underwater while lying on the stomach, back and in the sidestroke position.

Swimming the crawl with flippers
Doing the full crawl (arm stroke combined with leg kick and correct breathing) wearing flippers can give you a new experience, which will improve your style and above all give you a feeling of intensive speed when swimming.
Variations:
- Doing the crawl wearing one flipper, lying on the stomach over one or several lengths.
- Doing the crawl backstroke wearing one or two flippers over one or several lengths.
- Doing the crawl wearing one flipper as a relay race:
- Doing only the leg kick lying on the stomach.
- Backstroke crawl leg kick.
- Doing the full normal crawl.

Butterfly leg kick with flippers
Instead of kicking the legs alternately while wearing flippers, the leg movements can be carried out together at the same time. If this butterfly leg kick is done while the body is wriggling up and down then it is very effective.
Variations: See above.

Games to get used to flippers
The Water High Jump
Balloons are suspended at different heights from a line over the pool. Who can touch the highest balloon by doing a leg kick out of the water?

Variations:
- Who can jump up out of the water by doing the butterfly leg kick?
- Who can touch the balloons with the head?
- Can each member of a group touch a different balloon?
- Sweets are suspended over the pool at different heights. Who can pluck the sweets off the line by executing a leg kick out of the water?

Using flippers to carry objects
Objects (a pull buoy, a swimming board, a ball, an underwater polo ball) are carried along as a baton in the form of a relay race.

Stop and go
All the swimmers swim around on the surface wearing flippers. At a signal they all stop moving. On a second signal all of them go on swimming.

Variations:
- All swim with flippers doing the butterfly stroke.
- Doing 'stop and go' to voice signals.
- Doing 'stop and go' to visual signals.
- Additional signals given for different ways of moving:
- 1 x handclap = lying on the stomach, 2 x handclaps = lying on the back, 3 x handclaps = sidestroke.

Diving underwater with flippers
Diving underwater and doing the crawl leg kick lying on the stomach. The arms remain stretched out forward.

Variations:
- Diving underwater doing the butterfly leg kick on the stomach with the arms remaining stretched forward.
- Diving underwater doing the crawl leg kick with the sidestroke.
- Diving underwater doing the crawl leg kick on the back.
- Diving underwater doing the butterfly leg kick with the sidestroke.
- Diving underwater doing the butterfly leg kick on the back.
- Diving underwater wearing one flipper.

Pushing Competition
Two partners hold onto a swimming board so that it is between the two of them. They are on the centerline of the pool. Using the crawl leg kick they now try to push the other to the side of the pool.

Variations:
- Doing it wearing one flipper.
- Doing it using the butterfly leg kick.
- Doing it with two people at each end of the swimming board.
- Doing it using the backstroke.
- Underwater pushing competition with snorkel equipment.
- Doing it wearing one flipper.

Further games
Group pushing competition, Changing Direction, Swimming Wearing Flippers, Copy-cat Diving.

Catching games wearing flippers
"What's the time Mr. Shark?", "Chain Catch", "Fisherman, Fisherman - How deep is the water?", "Ox on the Hill 1,2,3" and other swimming and catching games (see RHEKER 2005 "Aquafun - Games and Fun for the Advanced" pp 69-73).

3.2.3 **The Methodical Way of Learning from the Body Wriggle through to the Butterfly**

Exercise 1: Doing the wriggling movement on the stomach
After the wriggling movement has been practiced in a playful manner with exercises and games, it can be concentrated on the movement while lying on the stomach. The arms are stretched out forwards like in the gliding motion. The head is held between the arms. The tips of the finger and the head start the wriggling motion and this is followed by wriggling the whole body ending up with the flippers.
Variations:
- Doing the wriggling motion with flippers over a width of the pool.
- Doing the wriggling motion with flippers over a length of the pool.
- Doing the wriggling motion with flippers over several lengths of the pool.

Exercise 2: Doing the wriggling movement on the back
The wriggling movement is now done as described above, but this time it is done lying on the back.
Variations: See above.

Exercise 3: Doing the wriggling movement in the sidestroke mode
The wriggling movement can also be done in the sidestroke mode. Lying on the right side, the right arm is stretched forward while the left arm is laid on the hip. The tips of the fingers and the head start the wriggling motion and this is followed by wriggling the whole body ending up with the flippers.
Variations:
• Doing the wriggling motion lying on the other side of the body.
Further variations: See above.

Exercise 4: Doing the wriggling movement vertically
An interesting variation of the wriggling motion is doing it with the butterfly leg kick vertically. Many children are reminded of the dolphin in the film "Flipper" when doing this. A good exercise for this can be as follows: Who can get up the farthest out of the water by doing the wriggling movement vertically?
Variations:
• Doing the wriggling motion vertically, where one hand is allowed to hold onto the edge of the pool.
• Doing the wriggling motion vertically without supporting oneself.
• Doing the wriggling motion vertically, where one arm is held up in the air.
• Doing the wriggling motion vertically, where both arms are held up in the air.
• Who can do the wriggling motion vertically and gets so far up out of the water that balloons (or sweets etc., being held up in the air) can be touched?
• Who can do the wriggling motion vertically, getting up out of the water and staying up the longest?

Exercise 5: Practicing the wriggling movement
First of all, leading up to doing the wriggling movement, the child may swim the style he likes best and finds easiest to do. When the child can swim a length wriggling with this stroke, then the movement is carried out lying on the stomach. This is followed by doing several lengths to practice the motion.

Exercise 6: Bringing a rhythm into the wriggling movement
While the wriggling movements were regularly done movements in the previous exercises, the leg kicks of the butterfly stroke technique are different. Bringing the two kicks together in rhythm is done by using the following methodical beats:

A large leg kick - a small leg kick, a large leg kick - a small leg kick, or in the beat of: one and two, one and two, where the first kick (one) is always accentuated.

Exercise 7: Bringing in the butterfly arm stroke
The arm stroke is realized by bending the legs that the upper body is able to lie on the surface of the water to give conditions which are simple and can be controlled. (see Exercise 8 in Chapter 3.1.2.).

Exercise 8: Combining the wriggling motion with the butterfly arm stroke
While wriggling through the water over a distance, one arm stroke is carried out at any point desired and then the swimmer carries on doing the wriggling movement. The number of arm strokes is slowly increased while at the same time the wriggling movements are decreased between the arm strokes until it is a double-tact beat and rhythm is achieved.
Variations:
• Swimming a length, two arm strokes are included in combination with the wriggling movements.
• Swimming a length, three or four arm strokes are included in combination with the wriggling movements.
• For every four leg kicks executed only one wriggling movement is employed.
• For every three leg kicks executed only one wriggling movement is employed.
• For every two leg kicks executed only one wriggling movement is employed.

Exercise 9: Coordination of the leg kick with the crawl arm stroke
While wriggling through the water over a length, at any point desired a crawl arm stroke on one side of the body is done and then the

swimmer carries on doing the wriggling movement. When the crawl arm stroke is brought into the double-tact rhythm then the crawl arm stroke can be carried on.

As soon as the double-tact rhythm has been correctly coordinated with the crawl arm stroke, this can be combined with different variations e.g., two arm strokes on the right side and two arm strokes on the left side. If a butterfly arm stroke is occasionally managed within this rhythm, then the complete coordination of the stroke has been achieved.

Variations:

- Swimming down a length, the crawl arm stroke on the left-hand side is continuously used in conjunction with the wriggling movement.
- Swimming down a length, the crawl arm stroke on the right-hand side is continuously used in conjunction with the wriggling movement.
- Different rhythms can be swum:
- Four arm strokes on the left-hand side and four arm strokes on the right-hand side.
- Two arm strokes on the left-hand side and two arm strokes on the right-hand side.
- One arm stroke on the left-hand side and one arm stroke on the right-hand side.
- While doing the rhythm of the crawl arm stroke (two right, two left) one butterfly arm stroke is included.
- While doing the rhythm of the crawl arm stroke (two right, two left) two butterfly arm strokes are included.
- While doing the rhythm of the crawl arm stroke (one right, one left) one butterfly arm stroke is included.
- While doing the rhythm of the crawl arm stroke (two right, two left) several butterfly arm strokes are included.
- The number of butterfly arm strokes increases and the number of crawl arm strokes decreases.

Exercise 10: Learning the correct breathing
For games and exercise forms to learn the correct breathing see Chapter 3.1.2. Exercises 14 and 15.

Exercise 11: Full coordination of the style with correct breathing
The rhythmical breathing needed for the butterfly technique is now coordinated with the other movements. First of all this is done over short distances. As confidence grows the distances can be increased.

Exercise 12: Full coordination of the style without the use of flippers
As in Exercise 11 above, but now without the use of flippers.

Exercise 13: Regular repetitions over short distances
See Exercise 18 in Chapter 3.1.2.
:
Exercise 14: Increasing the swimming distance
See Exercise 19 in Chapter 3.1.2.

Exercise 15: Improving stamina
See Exercise 20 in Chapter 3.1.2.

Exercise 16: Increasing performance using games and exercise forms
See Exercise 22 in Chapter 3.1.2.

3.2.4 The Advantages and Disadvantages of the Flipper Method

Table 3: *The advantages and disadvantages of the flipper method*

Advantages	Disadvantages
• Because the flippers give a lot of forward drive, less energy is expended doing the butterfly. This allows one to concentrate more on the technique. • The speed achievable when swimming with flippers gives one more experiences. • Swimming with flippers gives the pupils more motivation.	• Problems can occur when the flippers are taken off after learning the technique. • The second leg kick (done in the pressure pulling phase) is not as easy to learn as it is by using the dolphin dive method. • Because the flippers provide a strong drive forward, there can be a feeling that the arm stroke gives little thrust to the stroke.

- One starts to learn at a level where the movements are already known (Crawl leg kick and crawl arm stroke).
- The wave-like wriggling movement of the body can be learned easily and well as a basis for the butterfly stroke
- The flipper method is a comprehensive method to learn the butterfly stroke, where at the beginning the arm stroke is left out.

Other Methods of Learning the Butterfly

3.3

Program for Learning the Butterfly

3.3.1

The programman 'how to learn the butterfly stroke' has been developed by the Technical University in Berlin (c.f., BUSCH-KE/DAUGS/NEUBERG 1980). The basis of the teaching program for sports instruction can be found in the principles of educational cybernetics. In this teaching program, an attempt is made to use the principles of learning by rote using the sensory motor system. The theoretical background to this cannot be shown in this book. Nevertheless, the teaching program for instruction in the butterfly stroke, as used, is covered here in brief form.

The teaching program is divided into eight methodical steps, which are taught to the pupils at stations. Practice and instruction is done in pairs at each station of the program, whereas for each learning step about 6-10 attempts are suggested as allowable. The target elements cover partial movements of the legs, arms, the head and breathing. Those being taught are expected to work on their own. Independent work is encouraged in this method.

The course of instruction can be as follows:

- ⊚ **Look at the lesson cards and talk through the textual instructions:** The group being taught looks at the lesson cards and discusses what there is to be done.
- ⊚ **Practice one after the other:** Now both of the couple practice the program step.
- ⊚ **Joint discussion and corrections:** After practicing the step, the pupils exchange notes with each other and correct themselves helping each other.
- ⊚ **Test Station:** Teacher's decision: At a test station the teacher looks at the result of what has been learned. If the program step comes up to the teacher's expectations, they go to the next station. If there is still a mistake being made, the pupils can be sent on a "correcting lap".
  - "Correcting lap": Successful correction of the mistake, or...
  - ...move on to the next program step.
- ⊚ At the "correcting" station, the mistakes that are being made are corrected independently by each pupil. For this there are also the appropriate lesson cards.

Methodical Instruction
The lesson program for butterfly swimming is divided into eight methodical steps. Each station has the step listed in a text card as basic information. The pupils practice and learn independently in pairs.

P-1: Racing start
1. Push off from the edge of the pool -
2. - and glide with *stretched arms and legs* flat on the water.

P-2: Leg kick 1
Gliding along - and kick *both lower legs* up and down at the same time together.

P-3: Leg kick 2
Gliding along - and carry out alternately *a weak and then a strong* kick of the lower legs.

P-4: Arm movement 1
Gliding along - weak and strong leg kicks -
1. - pull the *hands downwards* as you do the strong leg kick -
2. - and bring them *under the water forward again* when you do every weak leg kick.

P-5: Arm movement 2
Gliding along - weak and strong leg kicks -
1. - pull the *hands backwards and downwards* (past the thigh) as you do the strong leg kick -
2. - and swing them *forward above the water* when you do every weak leg kick.

P-6: Joint practice
Repeat program lesson P-5 several times (at least 5x). Have your partner watch you that he can notice any possible mistakes. You also watch him and give corrections. After that have the instructor check the action.

P-7: Head movement
Push off - leg kick and circle the arms -
Lift the head *at the end of the arm pulling movement* enough so that your head comes up out of the water and -
1. - let it sink down again immediately.

P-8: Breathing
Push off - leg kick and circle the arms -
1. *Breathe out* hard *into the water* as you do the arm pull stroke and
2. - lift your head up out of the water at the end of the arm pulling stroke to breathe in.

3.3.2 The Advantages and Disadvantages of the Butterfly Learning Program

Table 4: *The advantages and disadvantages of the learning program for the butterfly*

Advantages	Disadvantages
• Comparisons can easily be made because the system takes place at different stations with everyone practicing at the same time. • The learning program is centered on the pupils. • The independent work format for practice of the exercises increases the pupils' motivation. • The pupils are encouraged to use their cooperative abilities. • The program uses well-known forms of movement (gliding). • The learning program is a comprehensive method to learn the butterfly stroke, where at the beginning the arm stroke is left out.	• Because the leg kick is not developed from the wave-like movement, but as a kick with the lower legs, movement problems, where the knee part of the kick comes in, can be experienced. • The arm pulling phase lacks information in that the whole phase is not fully described before (merely notes to „pull the hands downwards"). • The coordination of the leg kick with the underwater pulling phase („bring them (the arms) under the water forward") and with the butterfly swinging stroke („swing them (the arms) forward above the water") can cause problems because bringing the arms forward underwater takes longer than bringing them forward above the water. A problem with the rhythm can result. • The wriggling motion of the body as a basis for the butterfly stroke is not brought in or at least it is brought in too late as a penultimate step (P-7: Head movement).

- The method of programming the steps is not a genuine comprehensive one, because the leg kick is only brought in by using the lower legs and the wriggling motion of the whole body is neglected.
- The learning program method demands a lot of self-discipline from the pupils.

The Methodical Way of Learning the Butterfly from the Breaststroke

3.3.3

Introduction

Because swimming the butterfly stroke is similarly a harmonious double-sided stroke like the breaststroke, there is the option of comparing the movements with the breaststroke. There is a relationship between the two in their movements created "by axial-symmetric principles" (QUITSCH 1979, p 24), which makes it possible to make a simple comparison of the similar movements. Gradual changes made in the style of swimming the breaststroke can lead up to a close resemblance of the butterfly stroke.

This method appears, on first sight, to be quite clear and simple. However, when it is examined a little closer, problems do begin to come to the fore (see Chapter 3.3.4 "Advantages and Disadvantages").

The methodical way from swimming the breaststroke to swimming the butterfly stroke

The methodical way from swimming the breaststroke to swimming the butterfly stroke in the style of QUITSCH (1979, pp 23-28) is listed below in the following steps:

Learning steps:

1. Swim the breaststroke with more accentuation on the gliding phase.
- Change of format: In the gliding phase do an additional leg kick stroke.

2. Movement rhythm as in the first learning step.
- Change of format: The legs stay held together at the end of the leg kick: "strong leg kick movement by the lower legs, downwards and backwards"

3. Movement execution and rhythm as in the second learning step.
- Change of format: "Go into the gliding phase with more accent on the head and hands as they enter the water; coming out of the gliding phase the head and the hands come upwards again" (QUITSCH 1979, p 26).

4. Movement execution and rhythm as per the third learning step.
- Change of format: The underwater pull of the arms is gradually changed to be made longer as in the swimming underwater stroke. The hands are brought forward under the water.

5. Movement execution and rhythm as per the second learning step.
- Change of format: The arms are brought back forwards over the water.

6. Reducing the number of swimming underwater strokes in favor of using the butterfly arm stroke: First of all several underwater swimming strokes are done in conjunction with only one butterfly arm stroke. The number of underwater strokes is reduced, little by little while the number of butterfly arm strokes in increased.

This ends the methodical way of learning the butterfly stroke according to QUITSCH 1979.

The Advantages and Disadvantages of the Methodical Way of Learning the Butterfly by using the Breaststroke

3.3.4

Table 5: *The advantages and disadvantages of learning the butterfly by using the breaststroke*

Advantages	Disadvantages
• The program uses well-known forms of movement (gliding). • The methodical way using the breaststroke is a comprehensive method. • The pupils feel relatively sure of themselves when swimming because they (should have) already mastered the breaststroke. • Organization of the lesson is simple using a length of the pool, in case the beginners' pool is not available or there are no flippers.	• The methodical way of using the breaststroke is not a genuine comprehensive one, because the wriggling motion of the body is not touched on. • There could be problems with the leg kick which is developed from the breaststroke. There could be the mistake to have a 'knee kick' instead of a wanted butterfly leg kick. • The wriggling motion of the body as a basis for the butterfly stroke is not brought in or at least it is brought in too late. • The coordination of the leg kick with the underwater pulling phase and with the butterfly swinging stroke can cause problems because bringing the arms forward underwater takes longer than bringing them forward above the water. A problem with the rhythm can result.

3.4 A Combination of the Various Methods of Learning to Swim the Butterfly Stroke

Since each of the methods included above has advantages but also disadvantages, one should not become hard and fast only on one method when dealing with instruction and practice. Of course, there are a number of good arguments for the first two methods for learning the butterfly stroke (the flipper method and the dolphin dive method). Because the leg kick in the dolphin dive method almost automatically teaches the right coordination of the leg kick in the pressure phase, and the other leg kick in the flipper method, a combination of these two methods, dependent on the type of pupil being taught, is advisable.

Because the many disadvantages of the method of using the breaststroke as a methodical way to learning the butterfly stroke, one should only use this system in exceptional cases e.g., when there is only one lane of the pool available or there are no flippers.

Index of Diagrams, Tables and Photographs

Picture 13:   New experiences gained jumping with a canoe (F. Dunschen)

Picture 14:   Passing the ball overhead (U. Rheker)

Picture 15:   Relaxing with a swimming noodle (F. Dunschen)

CREDITS FOR PHOTOGRAPHS

Cover photos: Sports photo by Laci Perenyi, Meerbusch (Front); getty images (Rear)
Photos pictures inside the book:
See Chapter 5 - 'Index of Diagrams, Tables and Photographs'.
Cover design: Jens Vogelsang, Aachen

Page 59:   getty images
Page 203:   getty images/Digital Vision
Page 233:   getty images
Page 237:   getty images

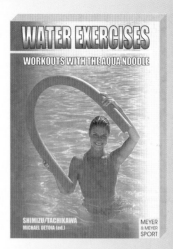

Lilli Ahrendt
Toddler Swimming

184 pages
Full-color print
96 photos, 19 illustrations
Paperback, $5^3/4$" x $8^1/4$"
ISBN 1-84126-164-5
£ 12.95 UK/$ 17.95 US
$ 25.95 CDN/€ 16.95

Shimizu/Tachikawa
Water Exercises
Workouts with the Aqua Noodle
136 pages, full-color print
33 photos, 108 illustrations
and tables
Paperback, $5^3/4$" x $8^1/4$"
ISBN: 1-84126-143-2
£ 9.95 UK/$ 14.95 US
$ 20.95 CDN/€ 14.90

Wright/Gilmour
Swim to the Top

136 pages, Two-color print
32 photos
Paperback, $5^3/4$" x $8^1/4$"
ISBN 1-84126-083-5
£ 9.95 UK/$ 14.95 US
$ 20.95 CDN/€ 14.90

Wright/Copland
Swimming – A Training Program

256 pages, Full-color print
30 photos
Paperback, $5^3/4$" x $8^1/4$"
ISBN: 1-84126-142-4
£ 14.95 UK/$ 19.95 US
$ 29.95 CDN/€ 18.90

MEYER
& MEYER
SPORT

MEYER & MEYER distribution@m-m-sports.com • www.m-m-sports.com

Uwe Rheker
Aquafun
First Steps

232 pages, Two-color print,
12 photos, 38 illustrations
Paperback, 5 $^3/4$" x 8 $^1/4$"
ISBN 1-84126-080-0
£ 14.95 UK/$ 19.95 US
$ 29.95 CDN/€ 18.90

Uwe Rheker
Aquafun
Games and Fun for the Advanced

200 pages, Two-color print,
7 photos, 9 illustrations and 5 tables
Paperback, 5 $^3/4$" x 8 $^1/4$"
ISBN 1-84126-163-7
£ 14.95 UK/$ 19.95 US
$ 29.95 CDN/€ 18.95

Barth/Dietze
Learning Swimming

136 pages, full-color print
24 photos, numerous illustrations
Paperback, 5 $^3/4$" x 8 $^1/4$"
ISBN: 1-84126-144-0
£ 9.95 UK/$ 14.95 US
$ 20.95 CDN/€ 14.90

Barth/Dietze
Training Swimming

152 pages, full-color print
26 photos, numerous illustrations
Paperback, 5 $^3/4$" x 8 $^1/4$"
ISBN: 1-84126-145-9
£ 9.95 UK/$ 14.95 US
$ 20.95 CDN/€ 14.90

MEYER & MEYER distribution@m-m-sports.com • www.m-m-sports.com

MEYER
&MEYER
SPORT